MW01168387

From Local to
Global

Smart Management Lessons
to Grow Your Business

EVAN J. SEGAL

authorHOUSE®

AuthorHouse™
1663 Liberty Drive
Bloomington, IN 47403
www.authorhouse.com
Phone: 1-800-839-8640

Published by AuthorHouse   02/16/2013

ISBN: 978-1-4685-6353-5 (sc)
ISBN: 978-1-4685-6352-8 (hc)
ISBN: 978-1-4685-6351-1 (e)

Library of Congress Control Number: 2012904874

Contents

Reviews

An Entrepreneur's Guidebook ★★★★★
Evan Segal's book, **"From Local to Global" is a must read, hands on guide for any entrepreneur who is running their own business, thinking about running their own business, or thinking about selling their private company.** Evan takes the unique practical perspective of discussing the "do's and don'ts" of managing and growing a business that frankly can be applied to any industry, addressing topics such as growth through acquisitions, hiring, marketing and importantly, how to think about your customer. The book is extremely well organized, with a powerful "Lessons Learned" section at the end of each chapter. "From Local to Global" should quickly become the entrepreneur's guide to running and growing a private company.

Robert Sarazen—Vice President, Goldman Sachs & Co.

Full of well organized insights ★★★★★
This is a well-constructed, well-organized, thoughtful and insightful work by a person who has been to war and clearly knows what he is talking about. Each chapter has lessons that are well worth learning at each and every management level; it is a paean to the entrepreneurial spirit and a testament to the power of world-class leadership. _

Christopher B. Carson—Director: Business and Tax Group—Cohen & Grigsby

Practical-Practical-Practical ★★★★★_
Mr. Segal has produced a very interesting and informative book. He writes from a practioners point of view. He provides refreshing insights into how a business truly runs and becomes profitable. His frame of reference is not

a large business, where most things have been figured out . . . but a scale that we all can relate to—one on the way to success.

The questions and challenges posed are just as important as the answers his firm arrived at . . . and the journey is a trip in itself—one that we all can relate to. **He takes the issue of growth from slogan to reality . . . providing a blueprint for success.** Thanks for this solid book- . . . a must read!

Dr. Charles Bishop, Principal, Coral Bridge Partners

Fascinating Read for entrepreneurs, business owners and students
★★★★★

It's very well written, concise and an easy read—and makes its point well. The author presents a fascinating story about how he took over at his company's helm and grew a small local business into a global market leader. He takes a mundane product (a stainless steel gas connector for the food service industry) that most of us have seen (but never given a second thought to) and weaves a great story around it. **Lessons learned from the book include a first-hand view of a roadmap on taking a manufacturing company to the next level in the face of global challenges.** It also shows how an innovative small businessman can flip a global challenge into a multitude of global opportunities! I highly recommend this book to aspiring entrepreneurs, businessmen and business school students!

Dr. Bopaya Bidanda
Department Chair, Ernest E. Roth Professor of Industrial Engineering
Department of Industrial Engineering, University of Pittsburgh

Great Read, Better Lessons ★★★★★

As a freshly minted MBA, it is great to read a book that takes many of the academic concepts I learned throughout my curriculum and applies them to a "real world" setting. From Local to Global: Smart Management Lessons to Grow your Business is not only a very entertaining read, but is also filled with valuable lessons for anyone involved in today's complex business environment. It is evident that the author shares his "lessons learned" with the sincerest intention of helping others succeed. I would highly recommend this book to anyone interested in the complexities of effectively running, and growing, a successful business—The pieces of this book are timeless and will provide insight and ideas that will be useful for many generations to come.

Brett Paulsrud, Senior Real Estate Analyst, HFF

Interesting small business story full of valuable lessons ★★★★★
Interesting, valuable book on growing a successful small business. I picked this up as an entrepreneur looking for insight to build and grow my startup—before finishing the second page, I was jotting down ideas to implement in my own operations. The book teaches valuable business concepts through the story of a small niche product growing into an essential part of commercial kitchens and homes around the world. The author does a good job combining the creative and academic approaches he used running the business, with valuable small business war stories. These include getting through the doors of heavyweights like Home Depot, fighting discriminatory EU trade practices, and even getting plumbers excited about stainless steel gas line connectors. Definitely recommended for entrepreneurs, business students, small/ mid-size business leaders.

Brain Magrann, Principal, Traversis Global Training LLC

Contact Information:
Email: evanjsegal@gmail.com
Website: www.evanjsegal.com
Facebook: www.facebook.com/EvanJSegal
Twitter: @evanjsegal
LinkedIn: www.linkedin.com/in/evanjsegal

Acknowledgments

I would like to first thank all of the employees, customers, suppliers, manufacturers' representatives, and other stakeholders who played an important role in the success of Dormont Manufacturing. It was their hard work, dedication, and teamwork that laid the foundation for our success. I would also like to thank Stacy Brovitz. Working together, we provided the leadership to support the dramatic growth of the business

I would like to thank my father, Jerry, for his wisdom and guidance and for teaching me the importance of a strong moral and ethical footing as the foundational elements in growing a business. He always told me to act like a mensch, a true gentleman in all my actions. Building on his solid support made it easy to do the right thing in tough situations. His guidance, influence, and steadiness led Dormont through its formative years and his invention of the stainless steel gas connector enabled the company to realize its tremendous growth and success. I would like to thank my brothers, the Segal and Phipps families, and all of our friends for their love, support, and encouragement throughout my journey.

Most of all, I want to thank my wife Tracy and our beautiful daughters, Tess and Ariel. Sharing the challenges and providing a constant foundation of love and support, Tracy has always been a true partner in my career. Our daughters grew up discussing "how many hoses did Daddy sell today?" at the dinner table. From attending sales conferences to posing for photos used in marketing materials, my family has always been an integral part of my success. I love you all more than you'll ever know.

Overview

Over a twenty-year period, I led the transformation of Dormont Manufacturing Company from a small family manufacturing business into a world-class global manufacturing organization. Building a strong, highly motivated team, we achieved a tenfold increase in sales and profits and created several hundred new jobs. We worked with our suppliers to introduce innovative products, create new technologies, and expand into international markets. I was able to energize the selling of a business-to-business product—making sales meetings, distributor calls, and company events something that everyone looked forward to. Using best-in-class skills, investing in automated equipment, and giving our employees the room to succeed, we built a highly successful manufacturing business in a very challenging environment.

We worked with a wide range of customers, from multinational food-service chains, large retailers, and equipment manufacturers to numerous food-service equipment, plumbing/HVAC, and catalog distributors throughout the world. Each channel of distribution and every customer provided an opportunity to learn about their business and to develop a mutually beneficial relationship. We were able to identify best practices and cross-pollinate them across channels, delivering valuable new ideas to our customers.

After successfully leading the evolution of Dormont from a small local business into a successful international company, I realized that I had learned many invaluable lessons along the way. Through a series of speeches to executives at national trade shows, I found that the knowledge that I had gained was relevant and applicable to business owners and managers. My goal in these presentations was to provide business leaders with some of the knowledge and wisdom that helped grow Dormont in today's challenging environment.

The chapters in this book address a range of topics, including growing and selling a business, creating exciting marketing programs and dynamic sales meetings, operating in a global economy, working with a broad range of customers and suppliers, and building the trusting and talented team that became the foundation for the success of our business. The stories/mini-case-studies contained throughout the book provide an effective way to both demonstrate and emphasize "smart management lessons". Each story was selected because it provided an effective was to illustrate an important management concept.

I hope that the insights and lessons contained in *From Local to Global: Smart Management Lessons to Grow Your Business* provide you with the opportunity to build and grow your business in a challenging global economy. I want to thank you for purchasing this book, and I look forward to hearing from you about your own experiences and ideas. You can find additional information at my website (www.evanjsegal.com), Facebook (www.facebook.com/EvanJSegal), Twitter (@evanjsegal) or LinkedIn (www.linkedin.com/in/evanjsegal).

Chapter 1
New Product Development

New products are engines to growth and profitability.
Exceptional performance in Product Development is the result
of a disciplined, systematic approach based on best practices.
—*Robert G. Cooper*

New products are often a critical part of a company's success. For Dormont, it was the invention of the stainless steel gas-appliance connector that fundamentally changed the direction of our business. This innovation dramatically changed how gas appliances are installed in two industries—residential plumbing and commercial food service. In many ways, these inventions impact all of us—whether it is through the use of gas appliances in our homes or whenever we eat in a restaurant.

As I embarked on my leadership role at Dormont, my challenge was twofold. First, we needed to capitalize on our potential for significant growth in the gas-connector market. Second, we needed to build a new-product-development team that could create innovative new products that would help support the future growth of the company.

I began by studying new-product-development processes that were being successfully used by industry leaders. After a thorough review, we decided to focus on a concept called a stage-gate process. In its basic form, a stage-gate system is a conceptual and operational plan for moving a new-product project from idea to launch. Stage-gate divides the process into distinct stages separated by management-decision gates. The company sets up cross-functional teams that need to successfully complete a set of related activities in each stage prior to receiving management approval to proceed to the next stage of product development. Focus is a critical component of a successful NPD process. It allows you to allocate precious resources on the most important projects. (If you are interested in learning more, in the appendix there is a list of references about stage-gate and other business processes mentioned throughout the book. You might also read about the NPD process at Apple that Steven Jobs used to create products that changed multiple industries.)

Another important tool that we used to support our new-product development was voice of the customer (VOC), a term used to describe the process of capturing a customer's requirements. It typically consists of both qualitative and quantitative research steps. Our team would work with our customers to produce a detailed set of customer wants and needs and then prioritize them in terms of relative importance and satisfaction with current alternatives. These were used as the key input for new-product definition and the setting of detailed design specifications.

We began building our NPD team by successfully hiring a group of talented engineering and marketing professionals who brought a great deal of knowledge, ideas, and enthusiasm. We were most successful when it involved an extension of our current products and other product extensions developed collaboratively with our supply chain.

The Invention of the Stainless Steel Gas Connector

Dormont sold a line of flexible metal connectors that were used to attach residential gas appliances. These were flexible brass tubes that were made in small sizes (three-eighths inch and one-half inch diameter) and in lengths ranging from twelve inches to seventy-two inches. It was easier to install a gas appliance with a flexible line (vs. hard pipe) as the connection could be attached to the gas supply at the wall and then the appliance could be pushed back into the space. The best examples would be a gas range in a kitchen or a gas dryer in a laundry room. Dormont began to purchase gas connectors and valves and sold them with our line of small Crescent water heaters. This arrangement generated additional sales and commissions, which made the Dormont line more attractive to manufacturers' reps.

After a few years, the number of brass gas connector returns began to increase. These products were used in residential kitchens and laundry rooms, areas where household cleaners containing ammonia were stored. The brass tubing was susceptible to corrosion from the ammonia, and this created pinholes in the thin-walled tubing. Eventually, the brass gas-connector manufacturers began to coat the flexible lines with a gray epoxy coating to protect against the corrosion.

As a result of the issues with the brass gas connectors, my father (Jerry) began to think about a better solution. Was there a superior product that could perform the same functionality and not be at risk because of corrosion? From the many custom pipe fabrication jobs that Dormont produced, Jerry had learned a great deal about metals that were effective in corrosive conditions. He wanted to design a product that would integrate a metal that was malleable enough to be fabricated into a corrugated, thin-wall tube and could also withstand the attack of corrosive chemicals found in the home. He knew that stainless steel would be an ideal option. Building on the current product designs, he worked with one of our strategic suppliers to design and develop the first stainless steel gas-appliance connector.

In addition to the product design, Jerry had to address issues related to American National Standard (ANSI Z21.24) for residential gas connectors. This was a national standard that was adopted under the auspices of the American National Standards Institute. ANSI had delegated the creation and administration of standards related to gas appliances and accessories to the Z21 Committee. This committee in turn created the Gas Appliance Connector Subcommittee, whose members included brass gas-appliance connector manufacturers, code officials, and individuals from various gas utilities. In addition to performance tests, the standard included a design restriction in the materials section that allowed for only brass or aluminum as metals that could be used in the design of a gas connector. Put simply, the ANSI Standard limited the ability of innovative people to create a superior product that might use a different metal. In fact, the existing manufacturers had a vested interest in maintaining the status quo.

After Jerry joined the Gas Connector subcommittee, he submitted proposed amendments that would allow stainless steel to be used in the design of a gas connector. These proposals met great resistance and numerous objections were raised. These manufacturers had been required to coat their brass gas connectors and were concerned that a stainless steel gas connector might negatively impact their market share. Jerry hired several technical experts, including metallurgists and chemical engineers, to prove the ability of stainless steel to be safe in the conditions found in a residential environment. They developed several performance tests that could be added to the Z21.24 standard, which addressed the concerns of the subcommittee and allow for a stainless steel gas connector. After two years of diligence and hard work, Jerry was finally able to convince a majority of the subcommittee members to vote for an amendment that would allow for the option of stainless steel to be used in the design of the product.

Based on the superior strength and corrosion protection of the stainless steel, Jerry developed a brand name for the product—Supr-Safe®. Dormont introduced this new product into the marketplace—the very first flexible stainless steel gas connector. This unique innovation would fundamentally change the way gas appliances were installed throughout North America.

The Quick-Disconnect Gas Connector

As Dormont began to make inroads into the residential market, more and more people began to hear about this new stainless steel gas connector. As the news spread, it created many interesting opportunities. The most important came from the McDonald's Corporation, an event that dramatically changed the future of Dormont. McDonald's had a large number of restaurants around the country. They were also starting to expand internationally and had established a position as the leading quick-service company in the world. One of their most important concerns was the safety and sanitation of their kitchens. Their kitchen design incorporated a number of large gas appliances, including gas griddles (for hamburgers) and gas fryers (for fries, chicken, and fish). These were large, heavy, stationary pieces of equipment that were mounted on fixed legs. It was difficult to move this equipment, and therein lay the problem. A portion of the grease that was generated in the cooking process was projected on the walls and the floors around and behind the equipment. This created a fire hazard, as it was possible for the grease to catch on fire. It was also a sanitary concern, as the buildup of grease could attract insects and rodents.

A senior engineer from McDonald's called my father and explained the situation. Their goal was to be able to mount the equipment on casters (wheels) so that it could be moved away from the wall and the area around the equipment could be cleaned. This would help address the safety and sanitation problems. It would also be easier to service and repair the equipment if it could be easily moved. The technical challenge was that these high-capacity commercial gas appliances were currently installed with hard piping. Building on the concept of the flexibility and strength of a stainless steel product, could Jerry design a product that would solve this problem?

Jerry immediately began to brainstorm about how to address the unique and challenging conditions of this application. The first step was the stainless steel tubing—he knew that they would need larger diameters in order to meet the energy requirements of the equipment. He determined that they could indeed utilize the larger sizes required to meet the higher BTU requirements of commercial cooking equipment. In order to provide the additional tensile strength to protect the tubing as the heavy pieces of equipment were being moved, Jerry decided to add a sheathing of woven stainless steel wire over the tubing. This feature, stainless steel braid, was used in larger industrial stainless steel hoses and would add an important structural element to the design. Jerry also wanted to prevent the braid and tubing from becoming a place where grease could collect and build up, so he worked with a supplier to design a plastic coating that could be applied over the top of the stainless steel braid. The smooth coating could be easily wiped down and cleaned, adding to the sanitary features of the product design.

Next, Jerry had to address the issue of the gas connection. How could a flexible gas connector be easily connected (and disconnected) without tools? Jerry thought of the industrial quick-disconnect assemblies that were used in factories and other applications. He met with one of the leading manufacturers of the quick-disconnect assemblies and began to work with them on a design that would work in a natural gas application. One of the challenges was that the seals and o-rings had to be changed due to the functional requirements of natural and LP gas. Since the initial volumes were going to be small and there were no guarantees, Jerry had to convince the quick-disconnect manufacturer to proceed with this design. They eventually agreed and developed prototypes for testing and approval.

This was a great example of an innovative, collaborative design process to address a specific customer's application. Jerry went back to McDonald's to review the design concepts, and they were excited about the impact that this product could have on their kitchen operations. The ability to make heavy-duty commercial cooking equipment "movable" addressed the sanitation, fire-safety, and serviceability issues.

Once the design started to come together, the next step was to determine how to address the standards issue. Since this was a new product (and application), there was no applicable standard. Jerry drafted a new ANSI Standard for "movable gas connectors." This proposed new standard was then submitted to the Z21 Gas Connector Subcommittee for consideration. Jerry enlisted the support of McDonald's and several gas utility folks who worked in the food-service industry to vouch for the importance and need for this product. After a few meetings, the new standard was approved. The new ANSI Z21.69 standard for movable gas connectors set the stage for the successful commercialization of the quick-disconnect gas connector.

New Quick-Disconnect Coupling

An important component in the Dormont movable gas connector was the quick-disconnect coupling. Jerry had to convince a manufacturer to modify their standard industrial design to meet the requirements of this application. This arrangement worked well for a number of years, but the manufacturer did not want to make any upgrades or changes that might improve the product. In addition, they began to compete directly with us by selling this new gas quick-disconnect product through their distributors and to our competitors.

As part of our process of upgrading and improving our core products, we began to look for another high-quality quick-disconnect manufacturer who would be willing to develop a new design that would integrate new features for food-service applications. We knew that the upgrades would improve the functionality of our products and help to further differentiate our products from the competition. In addition, we wanted a partner that would not undermine our sales efforts. We would be offering the manufacturer a significant amount of new business in exchange for a collaborative working agreement. We met with the owners of a Pennsylvania-based company and reached an agreement to develop a gas quick-disconnect for our applications.

Our engineering team began to work with their folks to design an improved product line. The first phase involved adding two important product features: a push-to-connect design and a thermal shut-off (TSO) feature. We then worked to obtain the required product certifications and approvals. We shifted most of our purchases to this supply partner and developed an annual supply agreement that covered pricing, deliveries, payments terms, material certifications, and product approvals. We also worked with them to ensure a consistent supply based on a Kanban system.

A Kanban is a concept related to lean and just-in-time (JIT) production. The word Kanban is a common Japanese term meaning "billboard." Kanban is a signaling system to trigger action. As its name suggests, Kanban historically uses cards to signal the need for an item. Kanban is part of an approach of receiving the "pull" from the demand. The supply, or production, is determined according to the actual demand of the customers.

Later on we changed the color of the plastic coating to blue in order reinforce the Dormont brand, which was associated with our "Blue Hose." This color differentiation helped customers quickly identify a Dormont quick-disconnect gas hose. Building on the success of the relationship, we began to further leverage our partner's technology and capabilities. Some of the initiatives included:

- **New Products:** We designed several new products for key OEM (Original Equipment Manufacturer) customers that integrated their smaller quick disconnects with our flexible stainless steel assemblies.
- **International Markets:** Our supplier provided us with a quick-disconnect coupling from their European operation that we had shipped directly to our UK distributor.
- **Value Options:** Our supplier developed a lower cost quick-disconnect option that enabled us to compete with competitors who were offering lower prices for products without our design features. There is always a part of the market that wants

minimum acceptable quality at the lowest price. Rather than just walk away from this segment, working with our QD supply partner we were able to compete on both the high value-added segment and the price conscious segment.

This supplier was an important part of our success. As you would expect with any relationship, we had our challenges—but we were always able to resolve our differences.

QDV Innovation

An important part of our continued success was our ongoing initiative to improve our product line. We listened to our customers, reviewed the information from returned products, and explored underlying issues related to the installation and use of our gas-connection products. We also were constantly on the lookout for product innovations in related industries and in overseas markets. In addition, our supplier partners were always an important source of new ideas and product innovations.

One area of potential concern in the installation of a movable gas connector was that it was possible for a plumber to incorrectly install a quick-disconnect coupling in a reverse position (in spite of warning labels and arrows on the product). If this occurred, when the component was disconnected and if the gas shut-off valve was also open, it was possible for the gas to flow into the kitchen, usually into the overhead ventilation hood above the equipment. While these conditions were extremely unlikely, we began to explore product ideas that would prevent this potentially hazardous condition.

A number of years earlier we had worked on a project that had envisioned a combination quick-disconnect coupling and gas ball valve (QDV), similar to an electrical outlet, for smaller tabletop gas appliances. It used a small-diameter outlet and a highly flexible gas hose. Although an Asian residential product existed, no one had designed a product for higher BTU applications that would meet the demands of a commercial kitchen. This was an important lesson about how great product ideas can come from international markets and be adapted to meet local market applications.

A Dormont combination quick-disconnect valve (QDV) product would provide us with a significant competitive advantage. We knew that we would need a manufacturer that could produce a high-quality product in a cost-effective manner. We also wanted a partner that had design capabilities, one that could help us create a superior product. After a great deal of investigation, we decided to work with our European gas ball supplier and a quick-disconnect coupling manufacturer that was located close to their factory.

Our product-development team discussed a wide array of concepts, performance requirements, and design criteria. Building on these collaborative discussions, the team developed the design for this new product. It included the push-to-connect and thermal shut-off features that we currently offered in our quick-disconnect coupling. We also selected a blue color for the handle to build on the color associated with the Dormont® brand. With this new design, the QDV could not be disconnected until the valve was completely closed. In addition, the QDV could not be reconnected unless the valve was closed. This new design provided an elegant solution to a problem created by an untrained installer.

We worked together with our ball valve supplier to gain the required certifications and approvals. To help support our innovation, we applied for and received a patent (US Patent #5,383,492) for the use of this new product with our movable gas connector in a commercial kitchen. This was a great example of how we solved a problem by building on the strengths and capabilities of our European supply partner. We worked collaboratively with them to develop, design, and commercialize this new product.

Supr-Swivel Fitting

While we had considerable success with our movable gas connectors, from time to time we would receive a returned product where the end fitting appeared to have been twisted. The best analogy would be a garden hose, where the end can become kinked and twisted due to a great deal of movement. When used properly, the quick-disconnect coupling would be disconnected when the caster-mounted equipment was moved. In observing how kitchens were cleaned, we saw that sometimes people assigned to clean would just move the equipment without disconnecting the gas lines. They would pull the equipment out and slide a mop in the area behind the equipment. This could potentially stretch the gas hose and create severe stress at both end fittings. While this might save them some time, it was not a good safety practice and not in compliance with the gas-installation codes and product-safety instructions. That said, it was a real-world situation, and we needed to find a solution for these tough installations.

We looked at a variety of swivel fittings that were used in industrial applications, but none seemed to provide the range of movement that we were looking for. We even thought about ball-and-socket joints (like a person's shoulder). And then one day, the answer appeared right before me. I was filling the gas tank in my car and looked at the fitting that between the nozzle and the end of the hose. It was a "multiplane swivel," meaning that it had a range of motion in two directions, allowing for 360 degrees of movement. Could this be the solution?

I met with our product-development team, and we agreed to explore the idea. I contacted Husky, the manufacturer of the multiplane swivel and spoke with the owner/president of the company. They had never made a fitting that would work in a natural gas application. I explained that it would have to pass a performance test (for a gas-connector assembly) where it would not allow gas to leak at a temperature of 800° F for ten minutes. Their product was made from aluminum, which would not meet this requirement. They would have to use another metal in their manufacturing process in order to meet our needs. They did not want to have to clean out their molds, which were used only for aluminum castings that were component parts of the swivel. In addition, our project would require the use of different seals and o-rings designed for natural and LP gas. After hearing all of this, Husky decided that they did not want to pursue this opportunity.

We had studied other products on the market and thought that the Husky swivel design would be best suited for our application. In an attempt to change the president's mind, I flew out to visit him to explain that tremendous growth opportunity for this product. As I discussed the potential number of units that we might purchase, I could see him adding up the numbers. This could be a substantial piece of business, making us one of his largest customers. He agreed to explore the idea with his folks. Over the next few months, our product-development team worked with Husky's staff to design, manufacture, and test this new Dormont Supr-Swivel for natural and LP gas applications.

One additional challenge that we had to overcome was the fact that since this was a totally new product for our field, there was no product standard. We worked with an accredited laboratory to develop a "desk standard," a way to design and certify a new product based on a laboratory standard. Our ability to have this product design certified to this standard and approved as a gas-connector accessory enabled us to market this new multiplane swivel fitting. We applied for and received a US patent on this gas-connector assembly (#5,178,422). We found that whenever possible, the ability to gain intellectual property protection enabled us to build a market for innovative new ideas and have some defense against competitors that would copy our ideas.

We conducted a beta test for this new assembly at a fast-food location that served thirty-thousand pounds of French fries a week. They had twenty French fryers that were in use eighteen to twenty hours a day. We thought that this location would be a good test because they had experienced ongoing problems with movable gas connectors. After a few weeks, they saw the benefits and were thrilled with this new design. We saw quickly that it solved their issues and knew that we had a winner.

We launched the new Supr-Swivel at the next NAFEM Show. We included a greatly increased product line that included a full range of movable gas connectors with one or two swivels, along with gas-installation kits that included the Supr-Swivels. The product received strong support from our distributors and customers and was quickly adopted by a number of multiunit food service chains.

Looking back, it was interesting that a great idea came from looking at products that performed similar functions in other settings. The idea of using a gas station hose swivel did not just come out of the blue sky. We had been actively thinking about the concept, and by either luck or coincidence, I happened to focus on the swivel that day while I was filling up my car with gas. I knew in my heart that this product would be successful, so

I pushed hard to convince the president of the swivel manufacturer to collaborate with us to make the Supr-Swivel. It turned out to be a big winner for both of our companies.

Internal Appliance Component Assemblies

During my leadership at Dormont, we supplied several products as part of a very successful relationship with a manufacturer of gas fireplaces. These were shipped to several locations based on a just-in-time (JIT) delivery program that we set up with their logistics group. Our relationship was threatened when a manufacturer of aluminum tube assemblies offered them a lower price. Based on the raw material cost, a stainless steel product would be more expensive than a similar one made from aluminum. However, stainless steel offered significant benefits in terms of strength, durability, and corrosion resistance. In addition, a flexible stainless steel tube could not be kinked, which would cause a flattening of the tube area and possibly block the gas flow. We knew that our OEM customer was under significant market pressure from products imported from Asia and that they were looking for cost savings across the board in order to remain competitive in the marketplace. A significant portion of their business was with homebuilders, who were focused on enhancing margins by purchasing lower-cost items.

The customer agreed to work with us to explore mutually beneficial solutions. We found that it was always important to visit the customer's operations and see firsthand how they ran their business in order to identify potential supply-chain savings opportunities. Our NPD team began to explore a range of solutions that might lower the cost of this assembly. A first step was to visit their factory, where we closely observed the manufacturing and assembly process, the packaging and shipping areas, and the inspection and quality-control processes. All of these areas provided clues about where to search for potential cost savings.

We initially focused on the separate components of the product assembly. Each connection was a potential leak point. The labor cost required to assemble these items was a significant part of the total cost of the assembly. Our team came up with the idea of creating a single forged part, which would eliminate the assembly costs for these items. We entered into an exclusive joint-development program with an upstream supplier to produce this new forged fitting. In addition, we developed a method to attach this forging to the tubing in our manufacturing process. Finally, we added a pipe-thread sealant to the end fitting on the other end that would save our customer time in their assembly process.

The result of our collaborative work with our customer and upstream suppliers was that we developed a completely new product that provided them a higher-quality assembly (with fewer potential leak points) and we were able to share our savings, thereby lowering their cost of acquisition. This allowed us to be competitive (compared with the aluminum alternative that they were considering), and we secured a new multiyear contract. Our customer was so pleased with results of the collaborative process that they asked us to continue working with their teams to look for additional areas for savings. We were looking at additional versions of this type of assembly for their other locations, along with other supply-chain options, including returnable totes and electronic data interchange.

This was a great example of how we helped meet the needs of our customer by providing them with an improved product at a lower cost. The work with our supplier enabled us to leverage their forging capabilities and reduced our development risk. Our team found additional savings by taking advantage of our processes to attach the end fitting. And by visiting their factory and evaluating their assembly process, we found methods to lower their labor costs.

We used the capabilities learned from this program to develop a new product line. It allowed us to attach custom components directly to gas tubing, eliminating extra parts and leak paths. This new capability reduced the number of components and the time it takes to install the gas train on an assembly line. As we discovered once again, understanding your customers and leveraging the products and services of your suppliers can create new business opportunities.

Design to Solve Customer Problems

For many years, we had tried to sell gas-appliance connectors directly to the major appliance manufacturers. They had viewed gas connectors as an "installation accessory," an item that if included would increase the cost of their appliance. In a highly competitive industry, they did everything they could to lower costs. So regardless of the benefits, they did not offer gas connectors with their appliances. They left it to the installer, homeowner, or apartment renter to select the gas-appliance connector that would be used to install their appliance.

The dynamics of this situation changed with the introduction of a stackable washer/dryer unit. What the manufacturer discovered was that these appliances were being relocated when people moved to a new apartment or house. The gas-installation codes and product standard stated explicitly that gas connectors could not be reused. A new gas connector was required whenever an appliance was moved to a new location. However, installers, apartment renters, or homeowners did not know about the regulation—or they chose to ignore it.

The appliance manufacturer was involved in several lawsuits in which a gas connector failed, allegedly because it had been improperly reused. They realized that the best way to address this issue (and reduce litigation costs) was to provide a more durable gas connector with the stackable washer/ dryer unit. As Dormont was the leading manufacturer of stainless steel gas-appliance connectors, they came to us to discuss their problem and see if we could provide a solution. Our engineering team met with their folks and worked together to analyze the situation. The combined team realized that if you could not prevent renters from reusing the product, they could design a connector that would work in this application. Working collaboratively, we built on the knowledge and market experience we had gained with our movable gas connectors for the food-service industry.

Our NPD team developed a special assembly for this application and created a customized work area, usually referred to as a work cell, for the assembly process. We supplied these custom-designed assemblies for many years under an exclusive multiyear contract. We worked with the scheduling team at their factory to develop a JIT delivery program, ensuring that they always had products on hand to keep up with their manufacturing assembly schedule.

Several years later, the major appliance manufacturer decided to develop a line of branded installation parts. Based on our relationship from the custom-designed assembly, they came to Dormont and asked us to be their private-label supplier of gas-appliance connectors. We developed a customized retail point-of-sale display and drop-ship program for their authorized factory appliance parts distributors. These included our innovative gas appliance installation kits for ranges and dryers.

Our effective management of this relationship created multiple benefits for both the customer and Dormont. We provided them with a customized solution that leveraged upstream capabilities of Dormont and our suppliers and solved a significant problem for them. We proactively managed the deliveries, aligned with their ordering history, to ensure that their assembly line did not shut down due to an error by their procurement team. Based on the success of the relationship, they came to us to develop and provide products for their new branded appliance-installation parts program. Finally, our proven performance record with a leading major appliance manufacturer further strengthened our reputation as the highest-quality gas-appliance connector manufacturer.

This was an example where our reputation and successful track record led to the appliance manufacturer calling us when they had a problem. They believed that our knowledge and experience would be helpful in working with them to solve this problem. Our ability to solve this, and many other customer challenges, further reinforced our position as the industry leader. The fact that people in the industry knew about our standing as an innovator and problem solver helped to bring us other new customers.

Lessons Learned—New-Product Development

1. **A structured process is a critical part of successful new product development.**
    We utilized the concepts of the stage-gate and voice-of-the-customer to guide the development of innovative new products. This created an effective process to evaluate, prioritize, and fund NPD projects. Focus is an essential element, forcing you to allocate resources on the most important projects.

2. **Customers are a great source for new ideas and market opportunities.**
    Some of our best ideas for new products came from listening and responding to our customers' needs. Our most profitable and sustainable products were developed as a result of a design solution that met the needs of our customers.

3. **Solving customer problems may lead you to innovative new products.**
    Customers' problems may be opportunities in disguise. The invention of the two crown jewels of our business, the stainless steel gas-appliance connector and the quick-disconnect gas connector, came from our commitment to solve customer problems and find superior solutions.

4. **Explore international markets for new product concepts.**
    Exploring international markets may provide you with ideas about new products, innovative technologies, and/or supply chain opportunities that may be invaluable to your business. You may uncover concepts that can change the future direction of your business.

5. **The relationships that you develop now may become important in future years.**

As I looked back on the history of Dormont, it was fascinating to see how relationships that we developed were important building blocks for our growth. Our relationships with well-known customers provided instant credibility in the marketplace, and they continued to grow and evolve. These customers would rely on our expertise and invite us to work on new products and design programs.

6. **Standards may be a critical part of business success.**

It may be critically important to become actively involved in the standards process for many reasons. Standards committees may determine which products can be offered for sale. Your competitors may use the standards process for self-serving means, seeking to block competitive products that may threaten their market position. While the standards process is often highly politicized, it is important to be an advocate for consumer safety.

7. **The ability to protect your innovative new products through intellectual property can enhance the success of your new products.**

Our ability to receive patent protection demonstrated the unique qualities of our designs, helped support our product launches, and provided the returns to justify and support our ongoing NPD processes. It is essential that you understand the strategic importance of intellectual property, for it may protect (or undermine) your new products.

Chapter 2
Strategic Growth

When a defining moment comes along, you define the moment,
Or the moment defines you.
—*Kevin Costner*

As Dormont continued to grow, we continually looked for new and add-on products that would help increase our sales. We knew that we were somewhat of a one-trick pony in that the large majority of our sales were stainless steel gas connectors. I began to think about several different methods to expand our product portfolio, including creating our own new products, acquisitions, buying from other manufacturers, and/or developing license agreements with other companies. I would walk the floor at industry trade shows and visit companies on my trips overseas to look for products and ideas that might fit.

The challenge that we encountered was that there were few truly new innovative products. Most products would allow Dormont to offer additional items as more of a full-line supplier rather than simply a manufacturer of gas connectors. These products were typically sold by other companies, and beyond service and vendor consolidation, there was little value-add that we could provide. One of our biggest dilemmas was in choosing between add-on products that would be complementary to our current line and getting into a whole new line of business. Ultimately, we were most successful when it involved an extension of our current products, often developed collaboratively with our supply-chain partners.

Strategy

In order to help our management team think through our options, we engaged the services of a Kepner-Tregoe (KT), a management-consulting firm. I had seen one of their principals speak at an industry event and was impressed with their processes. We began to work with the Co-Leader of their Business Strategy practice. While he typically worked with much larger companies, he truly enjoyed working with us because of our ability to effectively and quickly implement the strategies that we developed. KT has a very disciplined process that takes a management team through a series of steps to establish the baseline for developing a business strategy. Below is an outline of the KT process. For more information, I have listed in the appendix several excellent KT books.

Phase I: Strategic Intelligence Gathering and Analysis

A rigorous process to gather, organize, and analyze data on markets, competitors, technology, and past performance to ensure that the right information is used to facilitate good strategic decision making. Phase one provides an information base for strategic decision making and an agreed-upon set of assumptions about the internal and external environments in which an organization will operate during its strategic time frame.

Phase II: Formulating Strategy

A strategic profile of the organization is developed for guiding day-to-day decision making. This profile defines key strategic elements, including the basis for competitive advantage; the scope of the products and services that will and will not be offered and the markets that will and will not be served; the relative emphasis and financial mix of the future product/market scope; the source of new business and growth; the capabilities needed to implement the strategy; the business results to be achieved; and the critical issues (barriers to implementation) to be resolved.

Phase III: Implementation Planning

As a result of formulating a clear strategy, many projects emerge, the execution of which leads to successful implementation of the strategy. The creation of a strategic master project plan is the key output of this phase, providing a detailed definition of each project, sequencing projects, developing a schedule, and indicating the required resource levels for each project.

Phase IV: Implementing Strategy

It is the implementation phase of the process that yields the tangible results sought by all organizations. During this phase, planned actions are taken, implementation is monitored, and the plan is modified as circumstances change and the strategy is revised.

Phase V: Strategy Monitoring and Updating

Ongoing review of the strategy is essential for keeping the strategy relevant as a key tool in the continuous quest for success. Typically, executive leaders are adept at reviewing the operations and financial dimensions of the business. The strategic-review process is equally important. Activities include determining whether the assumptions upon which the strategy rests remain valid; assessing if the strategic direction continues to make business sense; and keeping abreast of progress toward implementation.

Dormont Strategic Direction

This strategic planning process required five days of offsite meetings in order to develop and agree upon a strategic direction for the business. One of the points that KT emphasized is that they do not know your business as well as you and your senior management team. Rather than them devising your strategy, they lead the management team through a process where it can develop and own its strategy.

As described by KT, a strategy "*is a framework of choices that determine the nature and direction of an organization.*" It allows an organization to focus its investment of resources (time, people, and money). The KT process includes the selection of a "driving force"—a critical part in the strategic direction for a business. A definition of a driving force is "something that accelerates an event into a specific direction." While KT had defined several different types of driving force strategies, our choice was between a "products-offered" and a "markets-served" strategy. A products-offered strategy would mean that we would build on our manufacturing, engineering, and design capabilities and develop new and modified flexible stainless steel products that might be sold in a variety of existing or new markets. In contrast, a markets-served strategy would mean that we would sell any products that our current customers might be purchasing.

After a significant amount of deliberation, we selected a products-offered strategy. We felt that this provided the greatest opportunity for Dormont to develop new, innovative products that might create a competitive advantage. Our primary concern about the markets-served strategy was that we would just be offering "me-too" products, not creating any real value for our customers. Now that we had decided on a strategic direction, we had to proceed with an implementation plan.

Implementation

We looked at the product-market matrix that we had developed for our products-offered strategy. In addition to our current markets of plumbing, HVAC, and food service, we included opportunities in automotive, medical, and industrial applications. On the product side of the matrix, we included a number of different types of flexible stainless steel assemblies, including expansion joints, automotive and medical products, and a wide range of industrial assemblies. The next step was to investigate various options to enter these markets. These options ranged from developing our own equipment and technologies to purchasing an existing business.

Product-Line Acquisition

Our most successful growth strategy was the acquisition of a competitor's product line. In the food-service gas-connector market, our primary competitor was a company named Avtec. They were primarily a manufacturer of utility distribution systems (UDS), a fabricated metal wall that provided a means to attach cooking equipment to gas, water, steam, or electric wall connections. A UDS system was sometimes installed in a commercial kitchen for convenience, as it was easier than running the utility service lines through a wall. Avtec was originally a Dormont customer, but the owner decided to manufacture his own gas and water connectors. They decided to sell their connectors to other customers and thus went into direct competition with Dormont.

I knew that the gas and water connectors were a side business for them. Over the years, their sales representatives and other folks had told me that there was little interest or focus on the product line. Avtec was mainly an irritant, as they sold strictly on price. As we later found out, the Avtec inside sales manager was compensated based on sales volume. Eventually, the owner sold the business to a large company that owned an equipment division. Shortly after the sale, I approached the president of the company that now owned Avtec. After a few months, he indicated that they were willing to sell off the gas-connector product line. We signed the appropriate confidentiality agreements and began to review the information packages that they had provided. We were surprised at some of their customers, including certain distributors that we thought were loyal to Dormont. The volume and sales numbers were consistent with what we had learned over the years. The biggest surprise was how low some of the prices were to various customers. We visited their factory and evaluated their fabrication equipment, which was very limited. Based on our knowledge of the market, we agreed to a price and quickly finalized the purchase of the Flex-Con product line.

Our transition plan was pretty straightforward. We sent out letters to the industry—and to the Flex-Con customers—announcing the product-line acquisition. We told the customers that we would sell off the remaining inventory of connectors and that we would then switch all new purchases to the Dormont design. We had a significant amount of manufacturing capacity and easily absorbed all of the Flex-Con volume in our factory. We developed new pricing programs for all of the Flex-Con customers consistent with our structure. For those customers that were not distributors, we referred them to Dormont distributors in their geographic area. Within three months, we had almost seamlessly integrated the Flex-Con business. There were several significant benefits to this product-line acquisition. First, our manufacturer's representatives were thrilled because we had added new sales (and commissions) to their market. Second, our distribution customers were happy because it had reduced the likelihood of rogue distributors offering cut-rate prices. Third, our suppliers were happy because we increased our purchase quantities. Finally, our employees were delighted because we had developed and successfully implemented an integration plan that added jobs and strengthened our business. It reinforced our position as the market leader and further affirmed their trust and belief in the company.

New Market Development

Shortly after I joined Dormont, I began to hear about a new gas-piping system that was being used in Japan. It was known as CSST, an acronym that stood for corrugated stainless steel tubing. I found out that this new interior gas-piping system was being developed and sold by the two largest gas utilities in Japan, Tokyo Gas and Osaka Gas. The goal of a CSST system was to replace the hard piping traditionally used to deliver gas in a residential or commercial structure. The CSST was manufactured in long coils and sold on reels. It was installed in a fashion similar to electrical conduit, where long lengths could easily be snaked and pulled through the walls and joists in a construction site. There were typically two connection points—one at the beginning and another at the end of the run. This compared favorably with hard piping, which had to be cut to size and a new connection added every time there was a change in direction. The new CSST interior gas-piping systems could offer significant labor savings and could speed up the time required to install gas piping in a structure.

Based on our reputation as a leader with stainless steel gas connectors, we were approached by a local gas utility that was interested in including CSST gas piping as part of a demonstration house. We worked with the gas utility and Osaka Gas to facilitate the use of CSST in their project. We learned a great deal during the process and decided to evaluate the potential of introducing this new product line in the United States.

One of our primary concerns was that the Japanese design was relatively easy to install, even for a do-it-yourself homeowner. Given the litigious nature of the US business environment, we knew that might be an issue. We also knew that in many areas of the country, licensed contractors performed plumbing services. One way to ensure that only licensed, trained contractors installed a CSST system was to require the use of a proprietary tool for installation. We thought that this would help ensure the quality and safety of the installation and would be preferred by contractors.

We developed a business plan for the introduction of a CSST gas-piping system into the American market. An important part of the plan was the invention of a proprietary fitting and installation tool that would only be sold to trained contractors. We developed a comprehensive training program with a firm that specialized in training for the aviation industry. We worked to introduce and teach market participants (code officials, gas utilities, distributors, contractors) about this new product system. We also discussed the benefits of a proprietary vs. an open installation system.

However, it proved to be a difficult, slow process in a market that was traditionally resistant to change.

In the interim, several companies decided to enter the US market by licensing the Japanese technology. They decided to utilize the "open" installation system, which turned out to be the method preferred by contractors. As these new competitors gained a foothold in the market, we realized that our proprietary system, which required an additional step in the attachment of the end fittings, put us at a competitive disadvantage. While we initially had high hopes for CSST as a growth opportunity for Dormont, we realized that it was better for us to focus on our core business. In order to support our rapidly growing residential gas connector business, we decided to exit the CSST market.

An important lesson from the CSST initiative was that being first in a market may not always result in a long-term advantage. There is a concept known as the first-mover advantage theory, which states that the first company entering a certain market will gain significant market share and be able to defend its leadership position from new entrants. In our case, we entered the CSST market as a first-mover, bearing extra costs and risks. We were also at a competitive disadvantage compared with larger companies that licensed the Japanese technology. Depending on the situation, it may make more sense to enter when the market has developed and learn by the first-mover's mistakes. A great example in off this concept is the creation of the iPod, which built on the Mp3 technology. Apple designed a superior product that was easier to use and the iPOD has become an icon.

Acquisition
Our most challenging growth strategy involved an acquisition that we thought would accelerate our ability to implement our new strategic direction. We developed a list of companies that might be potential acquisition candidates, including the benefits that they might offer and the likelihood that they might be willing to be acquired. Through this screening process, we identified a company (Flexible Metal Hose) that appeared to be a good fit. We had heard that the owner might be interested in selling the business. While there were certain areas of the business that were not a strategic fit, there were OEM accounts that offered significant growth potential. In addition, we had hired a sales engineer who had previously

developed several high-volume automotive accounts. He believed that there were opportunities for new innovative suppliers in the automotive and light-truck marketplace. At this point in time, the automotive market in the United States was strong, and many foreign manufacturers were building new plants in the South, near the Flexible Metal Hose (FM) factory location in Atlanta.

We completed the acquisition and began to develop a transition plan of for the business. We decided to operate FM as a separate, independent subsidiary. Our biggest concern was that we needed to have someone on the ground in Atlanta to manage the day-to-day operations. We explored hiring a senior manager from outside the company, but we wanted to have the sense of trust and control to ensure the operation was managed effectively. We decided that Stacy Brovitz, our chief operating officer, would relocate to Atlanta.

Managing the Change Process

It quickly became clear that the situation at FM was worse than we had originally thought. There were problems everywhere—with people, equipment, customers, suppliers, and antiquated processes. Over the next three years, we began to re-create the business from the ground up. We created our change strategy based upon the knowledge that we had gained at Dormont, including our utilization of Six Sigma and lean manufacturing methods. We positioned FM as an innovative company that delivered design-engineered solutions for flexible metal applications, which provided superior value in terms of reliability and performance. FM manufactured design-engineered solutions for a wide array of applications in engine, power-generation, automotive, petrochemical, aerospace and multiple-process industries.

One of the biggest challenges early on was that several major customers were not happy with FM's sales support or performance. Concerns included lack of technical support (product development, testing, and validation), late deliveries, and poor product quality. Almost every order was late, and there was little or no communication with customers. FM employees accepted this poor performance as a way of doing business. Our largest customer notified us two months after the purchase that they planned to drop FM as a supplier. Given the critical importance of these customers, Stacy quickly swung into a firefighting mode. He got on a plane and visited our largest customers. He met with the key purchasing and engineering folks and tried to gain an understanding of their needs and requirements. He worked with the team to put together a "get well" plan and worked to rehabilitate our relationship with the customers. He provided them with a time frame for the QS 9000 certification that they were beginning to require.

All of these efforts paid off, as we maintained most of the business and were given the opportunity to quote on a number of new projects. To further help our efforts, we hired a sales engineer and located him in close proximity to the larger customers. In this way, he was able to become close to many of their design and engineering teams, serving as an invaluable resource. We saw this as an investment in the value-added relationships that we were trying to build.

Our ability to quickly turn around the business and respond to the needs of our largest customer helped to save a portion of their business. When a key customer told us that they were dropping us as a supplier, we decided to work with them on an orderly transition. We could have responded by dropping the ball, which would have ruined the relationship. They saw how we worked during the transition and our efforts to address the issues that they had raised. As a result, they provided us with opportunities to secure additional business. A key lesson was that depending on the complexity of the product or service, it is more difficult for an OEM to replace an incumbent supplier than it is to work out a solution with them. The additional time and expense required by all functions—including engineering, quality control, logistics, and purchasing—may significantly increase the cost of bringing in a new vendor.

Fundamental Changes

There were two events that had a significant impact on our prospects for turning around FM—the business downturn at our largest customer and our lack of progress in the automotive/light-truck market. One of our largest customers was a major provider to the power-generation industry. In the first twelve to eighteen months after we purchased FM, their orders increased significantly. This was a very positive development, and we were hopeful that we could capture some of the flexible metal-assembly business that was being supplied by other companies. However, there was a significant downturn in the power-generation business, partly in response to the boom/bust cycle and speculation in the electrical-generation market. Large corporations (like Enron) had set up companies to buy and resell electricity, and when it appeared that there were shortages, the demand for power-generation plants increased. Seemingly just as fast, the demand dropped off and orders for large power-generation plants were cancelled.

The net impact to FM was that the orders from this customer dropped to almost zero. They had a significant amount of excess inventory, and it would take several years to get back to the original purchase levels that were in place when we first purchased FM. While this was fairly low-margin business on a fully allocated cost basis, it did cover a lot of overhead expenses. The significant decline in sales from this major company had a harmful impact on our cash flow and profitability. This provided another important lesson about the risk of having one customer represent a significant part of a company's business. If that customer's business declines or goes away, it can have a profound impact on your business. As the common saying goes, "Don't put all of your eggs in one basket."

The second blow in our efforts to turn around FM was our inability to develop new customers in the automotive or light-truck market. Perhaps naïvely, we had listened to the stories that the sales manager whom we had hired told about his successes in generating new business in these markets. The potential volumes mesmerized us when we investigated the markets for exhaust gas recirculation tubes (EGR) and other related flexible metal-automotive assemblies. Building on our experiences of increasing market share in the gas-connector business and leveraging our knowledge of equipment automation, we truly believed that we could successfully enter this market. We clearly underestimated the time, energy, effort, and relationships required to become an approved automotive supplier. In addition, our timing was terrible, as the US automotive manufacturers were on a downward trend.

As the FM business continued to hemorrhage money, we began to explore various options. We realized that it would take years to turn the business around. We eventually sold the business to a strategic buyer. It was painful to know that we had not been successful in turning around the business. In addition to the significant financial impact, the entire process had been a truly humbling experience.

Product-Line Expansion

Over the years, a number of gas-appliance manufacturers had asked us to provide them with small-diameter stainless steel assemblies to convey gases and fluids inside their appliances. We would provide them with our standard small-diameter gas connectors, just cut to a shorter length. However, this locked them into using our regular flare fittings. As we continued to receive additional requests from our customers, we began to explore this business opportunity in earnest.

Appliance manufacturers typically used rigid tubing or semirigid aluminum tubing inside their equipment. Flexible stainless steel tubing could offer significant benefits as an alternative to traditional pipe and tubing systems for internal appliance applications. Our NPD team began to explore the possibility of making smaller-diameter corrugated tubing. At that time, the smallest diameter that we manufactured was one-quarter-inch inside diameter. From our work with our OEM customers, we knew that many of them used tubing in their appliances that was even smaller (one-eighth-inch and three-sixteenth-inch inside diameter). It would require a technology breakthrough to be able to manufacture tubing this small. Fortunately, our team never ceased to amaze me with their skills, ingenuity, and creativity. We were able to develop the capability to manufacture the new small-diameter stainless steel tubing sizes (which we named Flex Tube™).

We created an appliance OEM design solutions team that brought together our sales and engineering folks to combine our knowledge of customer applications, product design, manufacturing, and component sourcing to offer unique fluid and gas-conveyance solutions. Our design solutions team worked closely with appliance OEMs as they developed new equipment, established new manufacturing platforms, or investigated cost-reduction options. We worked to provide application reviews—prototypes and production-ready assemblies that met customer driven lead-times and narrow design windows.

We continued to expand the breadth and depth of the Flex Tube product line as we developed new solutions for various manufacturers. Dormont's innovative flexible assemblies were integrated into a wide range of gas appliances. We discovered that Flex Tube™ allowed manufacturers to consolidate numerous tubing parts, or SKUs. The development of the OEM Design Solutions Team and the Flex-Tube™ product was a great example of building on our core strengths to grow our business. We were providing additional products and services to our existing customer base, so we had a familiarity with how they operated. Our product-development team worked to expand the capabilities of our equipment to create new niche products that provided value-added solutions to our customers. Finally, we created a dedicated design engineering/sales team to act as an extension of our customers, positioning Dormont to help solve problems and grow our business.

In an ironic turn, one of our gas fireplace customers relocated their manufacturing operations to a subcontractor in China. However, the Chinese company was not able to provide the small diameter Flex-Tube that has been integrated into the product design. So we exported products to China that were used in the assembly process. So we were a USA-based manufacturer, using USA-made stainless steel, selling products to China. This highlighted the market advantage of technology and proprietary processes.

Lessons Learned—Strategic Growth

1. **It is critically important for an organization to have a strategic direction.**
   Leading your business without a strategy is similar to taking a roadtrip without a map. A strategy will provide you and your team with a framework of choices for the allocation of resources. Too often budgets do not align with strategy. Using a structured process can be extremely helpful in developing your business strategy.

2. **A synergistic acquisition can have many benefits for your business.**
   There were several significant benefits to our Flex-Con product-line acquisition, including increased commissions for our manufacturer's representatives, market-pricing stability for our distributors, increased purchases from our suppliers, and improved morale among our employees. Look for acquisitions that provide real and significant benefits to your business.

3. **Do not allow your enthusiasm for a deal to blind your judgment.**
   We wanted to implement our revised strategy quickly and let our passion impact our judgement. This was evident during the FM due diligence, when I wanted to win over the potential new customers and did not ask penetrating questions. Performance reports and detailed questions about FM's operating performance might have resulted in a more accurate reading of the situation. A more sober approach to the due diligence may have caused us to rethink or restructure the deal.

4. **Don't put all of your eggs in one basket.**
   Be extremely careful about allowing one customer to become a significant part of your business. If that customer's business declines or goes away, it can have a profound impact on your success. Many companies are confronted with good/bad news of a potential business relationship with a large company. These can offer both huge benefits and risks. It is important to carefully evaluate your options and ensure that you have a survival plan if that relationship ends.

5. **Do not underestimate the challenge of entering a new market.**
   At FM we underestimated the difficulty (including time, energy, effort, and relationships) required to become an approved automotive supplier. In addition, our timing was terrible as the US automotive manufacturers were on a downward trend. While you may have an in-depth knowledge of your product, it can be an up-hill climb to develop and nurture distributor and customer relationships that are often critical for success.

6. **Being first in a market may not always result in a long-term advantage.**
   As we discovered with the CSST product category, being the first to enter the market did not ensure our success. We entered the market as a first-mover, bearing extra costs and risks, but ultimately did not have the best solution. Depending on the situation, it may make more sense to enter when the market has developed and learn by the first-mover's mistakes.

7. **Focus on your core strengths to grow your business.**
   The development of the OEM Design Solutions Team and the Flex-Tube™ product was a great example of building on what we did best. We provided additional products and services to our existing customer base. Our NPD team worked to create value-added solutions for our customers. And our Design Solutions Team became an extension of our customers, positioning Dormont to help solve problems and grow our business.

Chapter 3
People: Building a Great Organization

People don't care how much you know,
Until they know how much you care.
—*Jerry Segal*

I quickly came to realize how important people were to the success of our company. Your team is responsible for implementing the strategies of the organization, and they interact with your stakeholders on a day-to-day basis. Your organization is only as good as the people who are on your side. The human resource (HR) function is absolutely essential in creating and sustaining a platform to recruit, train, and nurture the employees of an organization. A great HR group can literally make or break a business. One of the keys to success of any organization is that you must place a high emphasis on people and ensure that the HR function is led and staffed by forward-thinking professionals.

Building an HR Department
When I arrived at Dormont, it was a small company with approximately thirty employees. As is common for many small businesses, we did not have policy manuals. This is not to say that there weren't rules and regulations; it's just that some were written and many unwritten ones were embedded in the norms of the organization.

As we began to grow, I had to devote an increasing amount of time to HR issues. I knew that this was important but also recognized that it took time away from other areas that also needed attention. Once we reached a level of seventy employees, we decided that it was time to hire a full-time HR manager. This person would manage a wide range of activities—overseeing the recruiting/hiring process, the administration of benefits, and responsibility for compliance with legal/administrative requirements.

We were fortunate to hire a person with a solid background who helped us build a basic foundation. She developed an employee handbook, which put into writing rules and regulations covering a wide range of topics, including benefits, vacations, and disciplinary procedures. As we grew, it became more and more important to codify the company policies. We also put in a place a more formalized performance-management system.

As we continued to grow, there were aspects of HR that were becoming more problematic. These included the need for greater leadership, the ability to recruit more effectively, and the experience in implementing new best practices. We needed the person responsible for HR to be more than just an administrator—we needed a "leader" in the business who could also be part of the management team. In order to support our growth, it became clear that we needed to hire new people who brought skill sets and capabilities that we did not possess. The ability to lead this process, to actively find, recruit, and hire talented people across many different functions, became more and more critical. We were also encountering compensation issues, as people would get annual increases not aligned to job content or responsibilities. We needed to implement a system that aligned pay with our increasing number of positions.

An interesting aspect of our growth is that some people were able to expand their capabilities to support the company while others struggled with the new challenges associated with a larger, faster-paced organization. While our HR director was doing a good job on the day-to-day tasks, she was not able to step up to the next level and be a leader who could support our rapid growth. Eventually, we agreed that we needed to bring in someone to manage the wider portfolio of HR requirements.

One of the finalists for a new leader for human resources was Mike Couch. Mike had a very impressive background, combining a strong theoretical, academic background with fifteen-plus years of hands-on experience with a leading steel manufacturer. He had worked at both the factory and the corporate headquarters, so he would be able to connect with employees at all levels. Over the years, he had worked with a several leading national HR consulting firms and had implemented a number of best practices throughout his career. He was personable and intelligent and appeared to be a good fit.

One of our hopes was that the new person would be able to lead and facilitate strategic discussions at both a corporate level and with our business teams. During his second round of interviews, we asked Mike to facilitate a discussion on a specific strategy. He quickly took control of the room, captured people's thoughts and ideas on Post-it notes, and then reorganized them, bringing order to the many notes posted on the wall. We were impressed with how quickly and easily Mike guided us through this strategy session. We were thrilled when he agreed to join our management team.

Integrated Vision and Plan

Mike had many ideas that could help upgrade our HR processes, but he took the time needed to learn about the company and to get to know the people at all levels. He held meetings with small groups of employees to assess the situation, listening to their concerns, ideas, and suggestions. Building on his knowledge and experience, along with what he had learned from these sessions, he began to develop an integrated plan.

A critical element in the design of our upgraded HR strategy was to create alignment between the business and all of the employees. We wanted to ensure that we were all on the same page and that our compensation systems aligned individuals with the company. This started with the overall mission and strategy for the company. As a management team, we had carefully and thoughtfully determined our corporate strategy. We decided to use a five-year time frame, and we would update and/or refresh the strategy annually. Using the strategic plan as a platform, we put together an annual business (operating) plan that included specific goals and objectives for both the business units and from the functional areas. We then wanted to connect these goals to individuals' objectives and ultimately to their compensation. This would enable us to align the goals of all of our employees with the business. Here is a simple diagram of our process:

Business Mission/Strategy → *Business Plan* → *Annual Objectives* → *Compensation*

Performance-Management Process

In order to realize this alignment, we restructured our performance-management process in a way that would meet the following goals:

- Focus work on business results
- Agree on goals and behavior
- Provide regular communications focused on goals
- Discuss career path and personal development
- Tie rewards to performance

We thought about performance management as a continuous, closed-loop, iterative process. The four areas—planning, coaching, review, and reward—were connected in an ongoing process that continued throughout the year. Rather than thinking about performance management as something that was done at the end of the year (often with great stress and agony), we started to view it as a continuous process.

A critically important concept that we added was that of "Success Factors." These are behaviors that are essential for success for both the person and the company. The concept was developed by a company called Lominger and was based on extensive research at numerous companies. (See the appendix for Lominger resource information). In order to achieve the desired results, we needed to add to our objectives (what work is required) the idea of behaviors or success factors (how the work is done). In their Career Architect® Book, Lominger identified sixty-seven success factors that may be important to success for a specific position. Examples of these include:

- **Planning/Problem Solving:** planning, organizing, customer focus, problem solving, process management
- **Working With Others:** interpersonal savvy, written communications, organization agility, peer relationships, integrity and trust, innovation management
- **Achieving Results:** action oriented, drive for results, dealing with ambiguity

| 35

We worked to integrate these success factors into our performance-management process. We started by identifying the top three success factors that were critical to the success of the company (such as customer focus). We included these in the performance plans for all employees.

The next step was to determine what additional success factors were critical for specific positions throughout the company. These varied based upon the functional area and the requirements of the position. For example, written and verbal communications are extremely important for marketing and sales, while process management and TQM may be critical for operations. This is not to say that written communications are not important for all employees, just that they have a higher priority in certain positions.

One of the benefits of using success factors in a performance-management system is that they can be refined or changed as an employee makes improvements, which are part of their individualized development plan. This plan might include special job assignments, 360 evaluation and feedback, coaching and counseling, mentoring, and coursework and reading. The Career Architect provides managers with the tools to help employees effectively develop the behaviors required for success in specific positions and aligned with company goals.

Market-Based Pay Grades

Another important step in the creation of our integrated performance-management system was the development of "market-based pay grades." We analyzed every single salaried position in the company and placed them in a series of salary grades (or levels). Each of these grades was assigned a salary range that had a minimum, a midpoint, and a maximum. The midpoint represented the market value—or average salary that a salaried employee would expect in a competitive market. This new system of pay grades also put in place consistent titles, which was important to ensure consistency across all functional areas. It created a defined career path, so that a person could clearly see future opportunities for growth and progression—either within their functional area or in other departments if they were interested. Finally, the salary grades became an important component in the determination of annual salary increases.

Performance Evaluations

We put into place a well-defined performance evaluation system that required managers to:

- Review performance vs. agreed-upon goals
- Evaluate progress vs. success factors
- Develop mutually agreed upon goals for the upcoming year
- Create a development plan that addressed specific areas where an employee needed improvement

A rating system with a 1-5 scale was put into place, using the definitions below:

1. Performance is below minimum job requirements. Does not meet performance requirements.
2. Performance not up to standard. Meets some requirements. Improvement action required.
3. Performance meets job requirements.
4. Exceeds some requirements and expectations.
5. Consistently exceeds all requirements and expectations. Performance is clearly superior.

One important feature of this rating system is that we were very cognizant of rating inflation. We emphasized that if employees were doing the tasks required in their job, they had earned a three rating. The manager had to have clear and specific examples to justify ratings that were higher than a three. In addition, we challenged managers not to give a satisfactory rating to poor performers just because it was easier.

SMART Objectives

One area that we also addressed was how objectives were written. Too often we found that it was not possible to determine if an objective had been met because of how it was written. At the end of the year, this often led to disagreements over whether an objective had been met. We were able to address this issue by making sure that objectives were "SMART," an acronym that stands for

- Specific: precise, exact, explicit
- Measurable: defined by quantity or quality
- Agreed to: everyone agrees to achieve
- Realistic: can be accomplished in the set time frame and with available resources
- Time-based: has a target date for completion

It is more challenging and requires more thought to write "SMART" objectives, but it goes a long way to ensure that a manager and his/her direct reports will agree upon the successful achievement at the end of the year. These types of objectives are also an important element in project management.

Annual Merit Increase

In order to determine an employee's annual merit increase, each year we developed a chart (similar to the one below). The amount of the increase was based on two variables—the annual performance rating and the current pay level.

	Current Pay Level		
Performance	Below Market	Market	Above Market
Exceeds	8 –10 %	5 – 7 %	3 – 5%
Meets	3 - 5 %	3 - 4 %	Lump Sum
Does Not Meet	0	0	0

On the vertical axis, the "performance" was based on an employee's annual performance review. For the chart, the numerical ratings were assigned to three categories: Exceeds (Rated as a 4 or 5); Meets (Rated as a 3); Does Not Meet (Rated as a 1 or 2).

On the horizontal axis, the "Current Pay Level" determination was based upon where an employee's current salary position fit in the range:

- Below Market: Less than 90 percent of the target market value
- Market: 90 percent to 105 percent of the target market
- Above Market: Greater than 105 percent of target market

This provided a clear, concise, and easily explainable model to award annual merit increases, while minimizing subjective judgments. This was a significant change from awarding an across-the-board increase (which treats everyone the same) or using some form of subjectivity, which does not ensure the fairness that employees are looking for. This model integrated two important factors—an employee's performance and their position in the range of their salary grade. It is important to note that if employees met their job requirements and were above market, they received a "lump sum" payment rather than a salary increase. We rewarded their performance but did not want to put their salary outside of the range for their salary grade. In addition, employees that did not meet their job requirements did not receive a merit increase—regardless of company performance. This new system for awarding annual merit increases helped to reinforce the culture we wanted to build, one where high performance was recognized and rewarded (and poor performance was not).

There were numerous benefits to this new performance-management system. It provided employees with specific knowledge about their current position (including base pay, salary grade, salary range, position in the range) and an understanding of the potential for career progression (and increased opportunities in higher salary grades). It also created a culture where employees understood what was meant by "high performance" and what was required in order for them to earn the potential rewards. Additionally, it also provided a system to help identify and weed out those folks who were dragging down the team.

HRConsultants

Over the years, we used several HR consultants who provided assistance in specific areas. As is true with all consultants, it is critical that you clearly define the requirements, objectives, and metrics for the engagement and that they are closely managed throughout the process. One company in particular, Lominger, added significant value to our processes. Their HR processes, including the use of success factors, were an important building block of our integrated performance-management system. We worked with folks from Lominger to understand how to utilize and implement their programs. Their books are useful tools for managers, especially as they work to create development plans for their direct reports.

Psychological Testing

One method that is sometimes used in the recruiting process is psychological testing. As we worked to improve our recruiting, we hired a consulting firm (PSP) that utilized a combination of testing and direct interviews. Their materials describe the advantages of their methodology:

> The first is that the assessment is completed by an outside third party, one who is not involved in the recruiting or the final decision making. Second, objective assessment provides a common benchmark with which to compare all candidates to each other. Third, objective assessment measures potential executive derailers such as poor decision making, energy/drive, emotional intelligence, resilience, results orientation, open-mindedness, and the ability to think on one's feet. These qualities are very difficult to assess in interviews and work experience reviews.

We had mixed success with psychological testing. On a positive side, it certainly provided independent, objective perspectives on the candidates. The interviewer was able to delve into specific areas of concern and provide perspective based upon the many interviews that they had done for other companies. Unlike our managers, interviewing candidates and uncovering positive and negative points is what they did every day. On the negative side, they could not understand the culture or fit aspects of our company. In addition, some candidates may have found the process to be intrusive. We found that the information was helpful but not conclusive. As you would expect, we ultimately had to make hiring decisions based on all of the information at hand.

Management Recruiters

For several of our senior management positions, we engaged the services of management recruiters. Our first significant experience was with a recruiter that we met through business contacts. We thought that he could attract the type of talent that could significantly help our company. Using a high-profile management recruitment firm is a very expensive proposition. The typical fee may equal the total compensation of the candidate for the first year. We had a very uneven experience with this particular recruiter. For the three positions where we engaged his services, one worked out quite well, one had mixed success, and one was a failure. I have mixed feelings about the effectiveness of management recruiters. They can be useful conduits in helping identify and bring candidates to the table. However, it is extremely important to conduct your own due diligence and observe the candidate in multiple situations. Don't be in a hurry to fill a position. Make sure that you deeply explore all areas that are critical for success in the position; utilize psychological testing and interviews where appropriate; meet the candidate several times (preferably in different settings); and create situations where you can see the candidate interact and work with your team and possibly his/her direct reports.

Targeted Recruiting

While at Scott, I interviewed MBA students from several top-flight schools. One interesting lesson learned through this experience, one that was reinforced throughout my career, was to not "overhire." The candidate might have unrealistic expectations about the position and the company, and this incompatibility might cause them to leave after a few years. These were high-powered programs whose students had very high career expectations upon graduation. They had read and developed strategies in "case study" classes where they were asked to act as if they were the CEOs of these companies. This reinforced the notion that they should immediately be placed at a high level, given significant responsibilities right away, and promoted quickly and often. This was an unrealistic belief of how career advancement worked.

New hires needed to demonstrate their skills and abilities and prove that they had the capabilities to move up the ladder. Advancement wasn't just handed to you because you were an MBA. Most MBAs at Scott stayed a few years and then left for positions in other companies. We invested a great deal in training and developing them but were not able to meet their often unrealistic expectations about career advancement. I recommended that we recruit undergraduates from Penn State, Drexel, Pitt, or IUP—hardworking, diligent, and talented young people who were less likely to join the company with inflated expectations. There was a greater probability that they would be patient, demonstrate greater loyalty, and be with the company for a longer period of time.

I have found that more often than not, you will have greater success hiring a talented young person with a solid GPA from a local school than an MBA from a top-ten school. This depends on the skill sets and competencies required for the position, but my point is that you need to be thoughtful about realistic career expectations when recruiting and filling positions.

Talent Management

One consultant that helped us think about our management team was Charlie Bishop. He was a person with significant experience in implementing management changes. Charlie had written a book about assessing change capacity within an organization. We found Charlie to be helpful in thinking about succession issues, identification of future leaders, coaching senior managers, and pushing us to make difficult but needed decisions about employees.

The culture at Dormont was always very paternalistic—we wanted to do the right thing and take care of our employees. If there was an employee who was having a performance problem, we tended to bend over backward to help him/her get back on the right track. Over the years, I failed to realize the negative impact that such employees had on their coworkers. After we decided to let someone go, other employees would come up to me and ask why it took so long. Didn't I see what a poor performer they were and how they were hurting the company? I came to appreciate the fact that my primary responsibility was to all of the employees and that I should not provide extra consideration and patience for one person at the expense of everyone else.

Charlie helped us to develop a talent-management plan, which included the development of highly talented employees and the transitioning of poor performers out of the business. As I came to better understand, if someone is not working out, it is important to make a decision in a timely manner and move on. In the end, you may be doing that person a favor by letting them find a situation that is a better fit for them.

Lessons Learned—People: Building a Great Organization

1. **Be careful not to hire people with unrealistic expectations about the position and your company.**
   This incompatibility might cause them to leave after a few years. Think seriously about hiring people from local schools or companies who have solid backgrounds and proven track records. They may reward you with superior performance and strong loyalty.

2. **The rapid growth of an organization creates HR challenges and opportunities.**
   Some people were able to expand their capabilities as the company grew. Others struggled with the new challenges associated with a larger, faster-paced organization.

3. **A structured HR program that aligns corporate strategy with performance management is critical to the success of an organization.**
   It is important to integrate elements such as merit-based pay, pay grades, and career paths. Incorporating "success factors"—behaviors that are essential for success—is an important part of a performance-management system.

4. **As a leader, your primary responsibility is to all of your employees.**
   Do not provide extra consideration and patience for one person at the expense of everyone else. If someone is not working out, it is important to make a decision in a timely manner and move on.

5. **A successful consulting engagement requires clear direction and close supervision.**
   It is extremely important to clearly define the requirements, objectives, and metrics—and then closely manage the consultants throughout the process.

6. **Selecting the right people for leadership positions is a difficult and yet extremely important business decision.**

When appropriate, psychological testing, management recruiters, and independent interviews can all be helpful in the process. Don't be a hurry to fill a position. Conduct due diligence and explore all areas that are critical for success in the position. Meet the candidate several times, preferably in different settings. Create situations where you can see the candidate interact and work with your team and possibly his/her direct reports.

Chapter 4
Climbing the Ladder

Management is efficiency in climbing the ladder of success;
Leadership determines whether the ladder is leaning against the right wall.
—Stephen R. Covey

At Scott Paper Company I was involved in several exciting projects, including the introduction of a product that changed a low-margin commodity into a high profile, profitable market leader; the creation of a national telemarketing center; the development of a business strategy to address warehouse clubs; and several product launches. I learned important lessons that were of great value when I took on a leadership position at Dormont.

<u>Changing the Dynamics of a Commodity</u>
One of my primary responsibilities was to compile, evaluate, and present regular financial reviews about our business unit. This enabled our team to see the regional profitability of our product lines. This process proved to be very illuminating because it highlighted for the first time certain product/region combinations where we were losing money. The analysis indicated that profitability could vary greatly based on the factory where the products were produced (some locations had lower manufacturing costs) and the market where they were sold. It also confirmed many of the beliefs that our team leaders had about product-line profitability.

One of the areas of great concern was our toilet tissue category. On the consumer side of the business, the Scott® brand was highly recognized and valued by consumers. This allowed our consumer business to build a highly successful, profitable brand. We were able to differentiate the product and increase the perceived value through advertising.

The situation on the away-from-home (AFH) side was very different. Since users in commercial settings (offices, factories, restaurants) never see the brand name, most of the people that purchased for these locations were looking for minimum acceptable quality for the lowest price. They were responsible for keeping within their budgets, so price was always a factor. Since we were not able to create any brand awareness, the product became more of a commodity. As our competition stepped up their efforts, the small profit margins of the toilet paper category were in jeopardy. In some territories, we were actually losing money. Our business team began to discuss how we could change this market dynamic. What could we do to change the commodity-like nature of toilet paper? Was there any way where we could add value to this category?

We had heard about a new toilet tissue product that was being marketed in Europe. It was a large roll of toilet tissue (the equivalent of six to eight regular rolls on one large roll). We quickly began to explore the viability of this concept in the US market. Our engineering team began to study if and how we could manufacture a large tissue roll. Could it be produced on our existing equipment? What was fascinating about this solution was that it was a "system approach." They were selling a complete dispensing system, including the tissue and a fixture. As we would soon find out, this offered significant benefits to the customer.

Our market research team conducted interviews with a wide range of purchasers and users to understand how people would respond to this new product concept. They also analyzed how toilet paper was currently used in commercial restrooms. One of the most interesting facts that came out of the research was that beside the purchase price, the highest costs for toilet tissue were related to theft and labor. The location where the highest amount of theft occurred was in women's restrooms. It appeared that women would take the rolls and put them in their purses. Given the high level of usage in many commercial restrooms, maintenance workers often had to return to each restroom several times a day to refill the tissue dispensers. It turned out that these two factors, theft and incremental labor costs, accounted for 30-40 percent of the cost of commercial toilet tissue. Both of these factors created a great opportunity for the large roll concept.

Unlike regular rolls of toilet tissue, the use of a locked dispenser for a large roll would eliminate the theft problem. Our plan was to create a giant roll that would hold the equivalent of ten rolls of toilet tissue, which would reduce the time required by the janitorial staff to refill bathroom fixtures by 90 percent. These savings meant that we could offer our customers significant financial benefits with a mega-roll toilet tissue system.

From a business perspective, this meant that we could increase the net price per sheet and still share some of the savings with our customers. This would increase our realized revenue, thereby significantly changing the profitability situation of this commodity-like product. In changing the sales dynamic by selling a system rather than just toilet paper, we were able to add value to our customers and increase the profitability of the category. This turned out to be a pivotal lesson: just because a product is perceived to be a commodity this does not mean that you can't change the competitive dynamic through product innovation. It also reinforced the lesson that many great ideas come from international markets.

Our team worked quickly to build a business case to proceed with this new concept, because we wanted to be the first in the US market. Our team developed a brand name—Jumbo Roll Tissue, or JRT®—and we began to prepare all of the materials for our launch. We began to look for high-profile locations for JRT to use in our marketing campaign. We successfully placed JRT in the New Orleans Superdome, and our team went there to shoot a promotional video. We interviewed folks who spoke about how JRT was making a huge difference for fans and patrons. On a whim, our advertising folks sent a copy of the video to *The Tonight Show* with Johnny Carson in the weeks leading up to the Super Bowl. They had remembered that Carson was involved in a famous incident called the Great Toilet Paper Shortage.

The Great Toilet Paper Shortage

It actually all started as a joke. Johnny Carson was doing his typical NBC *Tonight Show* monologue on December 19, 1973. His writers had heard earlier in the day about a Wisconsin congressman who said, "The United States may face a serious shortage of toilet tissue within a few months." His writers decided to include a joke based on this quote in Carson's monologue. He said, "You know what's disappearing from the supermarket shelves? Toilet paper. There's an acute shortage of toilet paper in the United States."

Too bad they couldn't see the consequence of this statement. The next morning, many of the twenty million television viewers ran to the supermarket and bought all the toilet paper they could find. By noon, most of the stores were out of stock! Stores tried to ration the stuff, but they couldn't keep up with demand. Johnny Carson went on the air several nights later and explained that there was no shortage and apologized for scaring the public. Unfortunately, people saw all the empty shelves in the stores, so the stampede continued. Scott Paper showed video of their plants in full production to the public and asked them to stay calm—there was no shortage. The video was of little help. The panic fed itself and continued. They finally got the shelves restocked three weeks later, and the shortage was over. www.theplumber.com

We got a call from our advertising agency that we should watch the Carson Show that night. Johnny said that there had been many stories about the Super Bowl, covering the players and their families. He then said that here was a story that the viewers had probably not heard about—and they switched to our promotional video. Our JRT® video was played on *The Tonight Show* for millions of viewers! It was a grand slam in the marketing world—and a great omen for a very successful product launch.

START—Scott Telemarketing Resource Team

With the rapid rise and impact of social media (Facebook, Twitter, etc.), the ability to use an emerging technology in market initiatives can be invaluable. This type of opportunity exists today in many companies, where a motivated person can help build a social media platform for their company. When I worked at Scott, social media was not developed, but I was able to use the new technology of the time to make important contributions to our companies success.

My journey began in a team meeting where we were reviewing the results of an outside "telemarketing" initiative. The product manager indicated that we were paying roughly $100 for each $50-case of product. This did not appear to be an effective sales method. So I said, "Isn't there a better way to do this?" The response from the product manager was "Okay, you're so smart—you come up with a better way to do this." The gauntlet had been laid down, and it was my turn to show them what I could do. I began to do research about telemarketing to learn how it worked and to determine how it might benefit our business.

Qualification of Leads: Like many businesses, our marketing managers "invested" a significant amount of money in advertising, trade shows, and direct mail to generate interest from both distribution and end users. These leads would come in a variety of forms—from magazines, trade shows, phone calls, and e-mails. There was no well-defined process to qualify these leads. A field rep would get a stack of unqualified leads for follow-up. More often the not, the leads were not very good. After going through a few of these, the sales rep would assume that the whole stack was worthless and toss them.

Since there was no follow-up mechanism, these leads (some of which might actually be worthwhile) were discarded. It was a bad process with good intentions. This seemed like a great opportunity for an effective telemarketing effort, where "all" leads would be screened and qualified before they went to the field. If a sales rep knew that each lead had good information, that the prospect had been screened and been sent information, and most importantly, that the prospect wanted to see a field sales rep in person, we could change the entire dynamic.

An effective telemarketing team could provide our field sales reps with a limited number of highly qualified leads. We could design a process that included a follow-up loop on every qualified lead with a method to determine the results/outcome from the sales rep. This would allow the brand manager to develop metrics about the effectiveness of various marketing programs. It could quantify the number of new customers, total incremental sales, geographical impact, and relative effectiveness of various marketing programs. While not an absolute barometer of program performance, a closed-loop lead system would be an important tool for marketing.

New Products and Programs: One of the challenges that our marketing manager faced was how to effectively introduce a new product or program. Our field sales reps found that it was difficult to get a purchasing agent to try a new product. Distribution sales reps were so busy—getting orders, chasing lost or missing products, and resolving quality, performance, or billing issues—that they did not have the time to learn in detail the features and benefits of every new product from every manufacturer that is carried by their company. So how could a brand manager effectively convey the features and benefits of a new product?

The use of a trained telemarketing professional was one solution. From a purely mathematical standpoint, a field sales rep can make six to eight calls a day. In comparison, a telemarketing rep can make ten to twelve calls per hour, or eighty to one hundred calls per day. Thus, a telemarketing rep can call ten to fifteen times as many people in a single day (and usually talk with 25-40 percent) when compared with a field sales rep. In no way does this imply that field sales can be replaced by telemarketing. Rather, when used in tandem, they can form an extremely effective team that builds on the relative strengths of each method.

Over time, a telemarketing rep can begin to develop a "relationship" with purchasing agents, engineers, and other specification agents. They can provide current, up-to-date information on products and programs. They can provide updated literature, specification sheets, and cost-benefits summaries. Working in collaboration with the field sales reps (and distributor reps where appropriate), this new process could dramatically improve the speed and effectiveness of new product introductions.

Distributor Customer (End-User) Calls: We found that our distributors were also frustrated with their inability to effectively introduce new products to their customer base (end users). We determined that we could call their customers (from a list that they would provide) and introduce new products on their behalf. We would get their approval for the telemarketing script and review the results and any issues/concerns/opportunities. This would leverage the efforts of their sales reps, accelerate the introduction of new products, and generate new incremental sales. It would also strengthen our relationship with our distributors and further differentiate Scott from other manufacturers. The ability to generate fees would provide an outside revenue stream that could help support a telemarketing initiative.

Scheduling Sales Calls: A challenge that field sales reps encountered in optimizing their sales time was the time required to set up appointments. The reps wanted to meet a series of customers located within a geographical area that would maximize the number of calls on any given day. The challenge was finding time with prospects on the day (and time) that worked best for the rep. It is a juggling process that reps deal with each and every day.

In addition, an important focus for Scott was to increase the number of calls directly with end users. Too often field sales reps would spend all of their time at their distributors. However, the decision makers for product selection are the end users. The ability to influence (and hopefully exercise some control to keep a distributor from switching an end user to a competitive product) is achieved by having a direct relationship with the purchasing agent and appropriate decision makers at the end-user account.

One way to support the field sales rep was for the telemarketing rep to schedule appointments with qualified, prescreened end users for our sales reps. They could tell the TR their geographic call process (i.e., Northeast on Monday, Northwest on Tuesday, Southeast on Wednesday, Southwest on Thursday, and office on Friday). Given this information, the TR could set up appointments with end users on specific days for two to four weeks based on the geographic calling pattern of the rep. This saved the rep time by working closely with the TR to set up future sales calls with qualified end users and prospects.

The Pilot Plan

Using the information that I had assembled, I built a business case to create an "in-house" telemarketing group. There were several benefits to an internal initiative:

- **Focus**: The employees would focus on Scott products and services exclusively, rather than being moved from program to program, essentially just reading a script.
- **Alignment**: We could better align the telemarketing team to the field sales efforts, as a dedicated in-house group could be trained and be sensitive to the issues, concerns, and opportunities of field sales. This would help create trust between the two groups and buy-in by field sales, thereby increasing the probability of success.
- **Collaboration**: We could create increased interaction, training, and support with the marketing team by locating close to the corporate offices—compared with a contract agency located in another city. Marketing managers could listen in on phone calls, help revise and update scripts and FAQs, and adjust programs based on results and feedback from the telemarketing reps.
- **Financial**: We would be able to closely manage the expenses associated with the program and eliminate the overhead and profit markups of external contractors.

In order to assess this concept, I proposed a small "regional" test for ninety days in order to evaluate the effectiveness of various programs. The next step was "selling" the program to the team. I selected the name "START," an acronym for the Scott Telemarketing Resource Team. It represented a new idea, a fresh "start" in approaching our sales and marketing efforts. Our senior vice president approved the pilot program, with one stipulation: I could proceed with leading the project, but not on "his time." He expected that the strategic planning and financial work that I did to support him and the AFH Team would not be impacted. I could use any of my "free time" to launch the START pilot program.

We set up in a room in the Eastern Region Sales office. The regional vice president and district managers were all very supportive. We worked with several distributors in the Philadelphia area who helped in this initial phase. The marketing managers were pleased that the leads generated were now being qualified and that we had a process to determine what happened to them after they were given to field sales. The field sales force knew that when we did give them a lead, it had been prescreened and was worth their time to follow up.

After ninety days, we evaluated the results of the pilot phase and determined that it was quite successful. There was a strong level of support, and we received the approval to expand on a national basis. START continued its success long after I had left the company. When Scott Paper was sold to Kimberly-Clark, one of the last offices that remained in Philadelphia was the START team.

This was an exciting opportunity that began innocently in a team meeting. I asked a question, and when offered the challenge to make something better, I took the ball and ran with it. As I think about the lessons learned from the START initiative, there are parallels with the growth of social media. Using emerging technologies, it is possible to reinvent your sales, marketing, and customer-service initiatives.

Managing an Emerging Channel of Distribution

While at Scott, I was able to work with Steve Sparkes to develop a strategy and business plan for warehouse clubs, which were a new, emerging channel of distribution. This was an opportunity to address a new method of retailing. Was it a commercial channel of distribution? They sold at wholesale prices directly to their business customers, including restaurants, small businesses, and offices. The warehouse clubs competed with traditional wholesale distributors. Or was it a consumer channel of distribution? They sold directly to the public and competed with traditional grocery store and supermarket chains. The answer to both questions was yes. Warehouse clubs were a "hybrid channel of distribution"—they sold to both consumer and commercial customers.

Our first step was to visit several of the warehouse club stores and understand how they operated. In addition, we worked with our marketing research folks to get a handle on why and what type of customers shopped at these new warehouse clubs and why they did so. We found out several important facts about how the clubs operated:

1) **Membership Required:** Anyone who shopped at a warehouse club was required to purchase a "membership." Consumer memberships were priced at thirty dollars per person or fifty dollars per family. Business members paid a higher price (one hundred dollars), but they received an additional 5 percent discount off of their purchases. This meant that the warehouse club generated a significant revenue stream before they sold any items. It also gave an air of "exclusivity"—only members could take advantage of the great bargains inside.

2) **Membership Mix:** Membership consisted of approximately 80 percent consumers and 20 percent businesses. This varied by location, and many business owners also purchased for the home needs using their business membership card.

3) **Price Point:** The goal of the warehouse club was to have items priced at a level that would encourage larger purchases and increased quantities of items. At that time, they wanted packages to have a price point between two and ten dollars.

4) **Pack Counts:** Based on the targeted price points, the warehouse clubs ideally wanted an exclusive package that contained more items than could be found in a supermarket—and fewer than are found in a full wholesale case. For example, a standard wholesale case of toilet tissue held ninety-six rolls. In a retail store, toilet tissue came in single rolls or four-packs. So the warehouse club wanted a package with a quantity somewhere in the middle, perhaps twenty-four or forty-eight rolls. They did not want this pack count to be made available to other channels of distribution.

5) **Boxes:** They wanted cardboard cases that they could take from the loading dock right onto the warehouse floor. A stock person would only have to cut open the case along printed cut lines and the products were ready to be sold.

6) **Distribution Efficiency:** The goal of the warehouse club was to cut out the unnecessary distribution costs that are embedded in both retail and wholesale channels of distribution. These cost savings would provide the warehouse clubs with a competitive advantage.

Business members were looking to buy items at prices that were lower than traditional wholesale distribution. Small businesses did not always want or have room for a full case of products. For example, a standard case of toilet tissue held ninety-six rolls. They wanted to buy a smaller quantity that would fit in their storage closet but was still at a lower price. The warehouse clubs could offer them lower prices because they did not have any delivery or sales expenses (like wholesale distributors). They offered business customers the ability to shop at "Business-Member Only" hours, typically from 8:00-10:00 a.m., which were less crowded. A small-business owner, a restaurant operator, or a nonprofit organization could come by with a small truck and pick up the items they needed at low prices. They were willing to shop for and pick up supplies themselves to save money.

Consumer members were also looking for lower prices—and they were happy with what they found at the warehouse club. A traditional supermarket would sell items in smaller quantities. They would unpack cases from the manufacturers, put prices on the individual items, and stock them on the shelves. For example, toilet tissue came in single rolls or four-packs. The warehouse clubs sold products right out of the cases. The items were bar-coded, so there was no need for stock clerks to label items and set them on the shelves. Since they were buying in larger quantities (compared with grocery stores) and there were fewer in-store costs, members were able to purchase items at lower prices.

Warehouse clubs represented a significant change in distribution. They were a serious threat to both consumer and commercial channels of distribution. This meant that the manufacturers that supplied products to these channels—like Scott Paper—would be caught in the middle. We needed to develop a coherent strategy fast, before the warehouse club customers would put us in a position that would harm our traditional customers.

The Packaged Products Division (PPD) of Scott Paper was divided into Consumer and Commercial (away-from-home) businesses. While we sold similar products (towels, tissue, etc.), the approach, style, and personality of the two businesses could not have been more different. It was extremely important to understand these differences in order to address this new hybrid channel of distribution. Our Consumer Division was a traditional consumer-marketing-oriented business. We competed directly with Procter & Gamble and Kimberly-Clark. We utilized a traditional brand-management structure and focused on marketing activities, including television and print advertising, coupons, and in-store merchandising. The primary customers included supermarkets and grocery chains. Our commercial AFH business was more open, freewheeling, and capable of adapting quickly to take advantage of market opportunities. Our primary customers were industrial paper distributors and large end users.

When Steve and I began to gather the facts, we found out that Scott Paper did not have a strategy. This was a newly emerging channel of distribution, and our organization was not structured to encourage internal collaboration. We had both consumer and commercial sales managers calling on the warehouse club customers separately. The purchasing agents were cherry-picking each for the best deals. In addition, our compensation plans were based on incremental business, so our own divisions were inadvertently encouraged to compete against each other. It was clear that we needed to work together as one company. We needed a coordinated strategy that built on the strengths of our company and eliminated duplication of efforts and self-inflicted wounds. We also believed that the failure to develop a strategy could have serious repercussions for our traditional channels of distribution.

We presented our findings and recommendations at a senior management meeting. We highlighted the operating characteristics and provided an analysis of this new channel of distribution. We discussed some of the dysfunctional internal behavior and the risks to our retail and business-to-business customers if we did not get out in front of this situation. To address these concerns, we recommended that a joint consumer/commercial business team be formed that would have responsibility for developing and implementing one strategy for Scott Paper. They agreed with our recommendations, and a team of senior managers from both business units was created to focus specifically on the warehouse club channel.

This assignment was an opportunity to learn about a new, emerging channel of business. The business model represented a disruptive innovation in distribution and caused all players in the supply chain to react and adjust their business strategies. The ability to understand customer willingness to go to a large warehouse and forego certain services (deliveries, shelf stocking) to get lower prices rocked the traditional retailers and wholesale distributors. We were able to play an important role early on in highlighting the importance of this development and working with the senior leadership at Scott to develop an integrated, collaborative approach.

Product Launches
WypAll®

One of my first experiences in changing a brand occurred when we developed a pop-up dispenser box for our proprietary WypAll® and EconoLine™ products. This provided an easy and convenient way for a person to grab a wiper with one hand. This was a significant step in expanding the product line and creating new sales opportunities.

I developed the capital job request for the new packaging equipment that we were recommending for our Wisconsin facility. One of the key variables was the efficiency of the machine. Our proposed package would have one hundred wipers in each box, with nine boxes per case (or nine hundred wipers per case). Our engineers recommended an automated process, which significantly increased the capital expense. This contrasted with a lower-cost option that would have required more manual labor. After a number of discussions, we agreed to proceed with the more expensive, highly automated plan. We closely tracked the operating performance of the new automated equipment, including productivity rate and manufacturing costs. After about a year, we determined that the equipment was not able to meet the targeted efficiency rates. This had a significant impact on the total cost of the boxed wipers.

Shortly after the launch, our competitors introduced a case with eight hundred wipers. They were selling it a lower price per wiper—and several dollars lower per case (thirty dollars vs. twenty-four dollars). Our sales folks tried to explain the math to customers, but they were fixated on the price point per case. When we asked our engineering folks about the possibility of switching to an eight-hundred-count case, we were told that the new automated packaging equipment could not be adjusted—it was designed to assemble only nine-hundred-count cases (nine boxes). This was another lesson. By their nature, engineers like to work on new, cool stuff. It is much more fun to work on a newly designed automated machine than to build a manual process. However, an automated manufacturing or packaging process may not always the best option. It may not achieve the targeted production goals and may sacrifice the flexibility needed to adjust to changes in the market.

Scott Wiping Cloths™

I was assigned the responsibility of boosting our wiper sales in nontraditional markets. It always occurred to me that many people outside of our industry had no idea what a WypAll® wiper was or how they could use it. This reflected our "commercial" bias (vs. retail), as our products were purchased and utilized in business settings (factory, office building, etc.). I observed that other manufacturers often used four-color graphics on their packaging, which helped to sell the product. Building on this idea, I worked with our design team to create a color label for the pop-up boxes. These included pictures of people using the disposable wipers in various settings (an automotive shop, a bathroom, at home, a factory, etc.).

We changed the product's name from WypAll® to Scott ® Wiping Cloths and packaged the boxes in a cut case that could be easily opened so that the products could be sold out of the box. These might seem like simple changes, but they had a significant impact on sales. Our customers in nontraditional channels of distribution—automotive parts, DIY home improvement centers, and warehouse clubs—now had a product that consumers could instantly understand and realize where to use. This was a great lesson on how packaging can have a major impact on sales. It can affect how a product is perceived and can provide a quick tutorial on how and where an end user can utilize your product.

ScottCloth™

I played an active role in the development, commercialization, and launch of ScottCloth®, a revolutionary new product made by combining cloth fibers with paper pulp to create a stronger, more durable wiper. Our primary competitors in the wiper business were shop towels, rags, and other brands of disposable wipers. The primary negative that end users had with using a disposable wiper was that it was not durable like a cloth towel. In order to address this, the wiper business had looked at a variety of product options over the years. Our proprietary technology resulted in the creation on WypAll®, a durable paper-based wiper. We also offered a product that had a plastic-type netting sandwiched between two layers of paper wiper. We explored thicker options, different pulps, and other chemical additives that might add additional strength.

Our NPD team developed the idea of adding cloth fibers into the mixing chamber of a paper machine. This allowed the cloth fibers to bond with the paper fibers, thereby creating a stronger, more durable product. We were excited about the idea of having a disposable wiper that could compete head-on with cloth-shop towels. We decided on an orange color for this new product to emphasize its cloth-like appearance.

We developed a brand name that would capture the essence of this new wiper—ScottCloth®. It emphasized the Scott Brand and the fact that this was indeed a cloth-like disposable wiper. Our team developed a comprehensive launch plan, including an innovative video that showed Benjamin Franklin with a series of new inventions. The use of Franklin's image reinforced both his innovative ability and his Philadelphia connections. It was a wonderful opportunity to participate in the development of a new technology and the commercialization of an innovative new product. It also highlighted the benefits of thinking outside the box from a technology standpoint.

Lessons Learned—Climbing the Ladder

1) **Innovation and technology can add value to commodity-like products.**
   As I found out with the JRT product launch, just because a product is perceived to be a commodity this does not mean that you can't change the competitive dynamic through product innovation. It also reinforced the lesson that great ideas can come from international markets.

2) **New assignments can create career-growth opportunities for high-potential employees.**
   When offered the challenge to improve our direct-marketing programs, I created and built a national telemarketing center. This leveraged the efforts of our marketing and field sales teams. This is the type of career-building opportunity that you can provide for high-potential employees who need to develop additional skills and experiences.

3) **New technologies, such as Social Media, can be an important tool to leverage sales and marketing efforts.**
   The START telemarketing initiative utilized emerging technologies to complement the business, including lead qualification, new product introductions, and optimizing field sales calls. This provided an example of how a new technology can be adapted to help achieve business goals. The emergence of social media platforms has created new opportunities for businesses to figure out how an emerging technology can align with their strategic goals.

4) **Channel innovations can radically affect the status quo, creating opportunities and challenges for market participants.**
   Warehouse clubs represented a disruptive force in both retail and wholesale distribution. The emergence of this new channel has caused all players in the supply chain to react and adjust their business strategies. It is important to recognize and react quickly to a fundamental market shift. Developing an integrated corporate strategy will position your company to capitalize on this new market dynamics.

5) **New technology and innovations create wonderful business-growth opportunities.**

With ScottCloth® and JRT®, we realized significant benefits by thinking outside the box from a technology standpoint and trying new ideas. The development and commercialization of an innovative new product can create great learning opportunities for both the business and the people involved in the project.

6) **Be cautious of automated capital equipment projects with bells and whistles.**

It is much more fun for engineers to work on a newly designed automated machine than to build a manual-type process. However, an automated manufacturing or packaging process may not always the best option. It may not achieve the targeted goals and may sacrifice flexibility that may be needed due to changes in the market.

7) **Changes in packaging can have a major impact on the sales of a product.**

The creation of a four-color dispensing box with color photos enabled consumers to instantly understand what the product was and where they could use it. It can provide a quick tutorial on how and where an end user can utilize your product.

Chapter 5
International Partnerships

By "flat" I did not mean that the world is getting equal. I said that more
people in more places can now compete, connect and collaborate with equal
power and equal tools than ever before.
—Thomas Friedman

An important part of the growth of Dormont came as a result of relationships
developed with international businesses. Several of these companies became
key suppliers that helped us launch and build our gas-connector business.
They became strategic partners in our supply chain, helping us add value
for our customers, resulting in the dramatic growth of our business.

Japan
Dormont developed a strategic relationship with a Japanese company
well before it became the "in" thing to do. This was a business relationship
that grew over a thirty-five-year period. My father and Yoshiro Misumida
(Chairman of Tofle, Inc) were able to transcend cultural and communication
barriers to develop a relationship, built on respect and friendship, that
greatly benefited both companies.

After Jerry developed the idea for a flexible stainless steel gas connector,
he began to look for companies that could manufacture the tubing in small
diameters. This would enable him to create a product that was superior
but functionally comparable to the epoxy-coated brass connectors that
were currently being sold. There were companies in the United States that
made stainless steel tubing, but none that made it in the smaller diameters.
By luck or providence, he received a letter from Yoshiro Misumida. He
had learned about Dormont and wanted to know if Jerry was interested

in flexible stainless steel tubing. Misumida contacted Jerry right at the time when he was looking for a new solution. Misumida's company, Tofle, manufactured flexible stainless steel tubing and assemblies. They provided samples for testing, which Dormont used to produce the first stainless steel gas connector.

Jerry and Misumida put together a supply agreement under which Dormont would purchase precut lengths of stainless steel tubing. We then attached the end fittings and assembled the complete gas connectors at our factory. As Japanese products (automobiles, electronics, etc.) grew more popular in the United States, the dollar-yen exchange rate began to change. This had a net impact of increasing the cost of the stainless steel tubing that we were buying from Japan. In a sign of great foresight and mutual confidence, Jerry and Misumida agreed to set up a joint venture that would manufacture the tubing in the United States.

I made several trips to Japan and developed a nice relationship with the president of Tofle. I became increasingly interested in quality-management systems and the Toyota Production System, which served as the basis for lean manufacturing. Back in the United States, I also had the opportunity to get to know Jim Womack, the founder of the Lean Enterprise Institute. We began to aggressively utilize lean principles throughout our factory to improve our processes and lower costs.

We eventually purchased Tofle's joint venture stake. It was with mixed emotions that we finalized the agreement. On Misumida's last visit to our factory, he told my father that as a result of our engineering and technical advances, "the student had surpassed the teacher." We were very proud of what we had accomplished with the support and admiration that developed over a thirty-five-year friendship. Over many years of our relationship, we developed a deep appreciation for the cultural and religious traditions of our Japanese partners.

Cimberio—European Supply Partner
As our residential gas-appliance connector business continued to grow, our sales of brass gas ball valves also increased. At that time, most of the gas ball shut-off valves sold in the United States came from Italy. The largest Italian manufacturer of small gas ball valves had set up five master

distributors in the United States, including our primary gas-connector competitor. This put us at a competitive disadvantage. We asked them if we could purchase directly so that we could be on equal footing with our competitor. After our requests were rejected, I knew that we had to find another supplier that would sell to us directly.

I arranged to attend, along with Jack Stein (our vice president of sales), the leading European HVAC exhibition. The goal was to find a world-class supplier of brass gas ball valves that would allow us to effectively compete in the market. Near the end of the second day, we were fortunate to meet with a firm named Cimberio, a valve-manufacturing company located in northern Italy.

We met with Roberto Cimberio and immediately hit it off. For Roberto, this represented an opportunity to develop a significant new customer. They were not selling any products in America, so this represented an excellent business opportunity. For Dormont, this would enable us to purchase gas ball valves at a price point that would enable us to effectively compete in the gas-connector business. We explained that we were a dynamic, growing manufacturer that could offer Cimberio an entrée into the US/Canadian market through an exclusive supply arrangement. They invited us to come to Italy to continue our discussions and to lay out in detail the types and quantities of gas ball valves that we were looking to purchase. We were excited about this opportunity, feeling that we had finally found a high-quality ball valve manufacturer that would work directly with Dormont. We quickly finalized the details of our supply agreement.

This began one of my most favorite business relationships. We steadily increased our purchases from Cimberio as our gas connector business continued to expand. I visited Roberto in Italy many times, including two trips with my family. We also began to develop several new innovative products, including a combination quick-disconnect shutoff valve (QDV). It was a business and personal relationship that was successful, enjoyable and memorable!

Mechline

Our position in the United Kingdom was in great peril as a result of a series of trade barriers that were put into place (see chapter 9: International

Market Access). We needed to find a UK company that was actively involved in the food-service (catering) industry and had the technical knowledge, skills, and willingness to help us fight the standards battle. We knew that we had a superior product—we just needed to overcome the stranglehold that the competitors had on the standards approval process.

In another turn of good fortune, we were introduced to Peter Sage-Passant, the founder of Mechline Developments Ltd. Peter was an industrious, friendly, ingenious, and hard-working engineer who had the courage to leave the safety of a large company and start up his own business. Peter had observed the difficulty in cleaning a commercial kitchen, especially with the equipment fixed into place. It was both a fire hazard and a sanitation nightmare. So Peter invented a brilliant system that enabled sinks (and other types of equipment) to be mounted on wheels. The equipment could be easily detached (with a docking-type system) and moved away from the walls for a proper cleaning. Mechline was just beginning to have some success, but the jobs tended to be customized and on a project-by-project basis. Peter was looking for another product, hopefully complementary, that would be an off-the-shelf product line that would offer a more consistent baseline level of sales.

The Dormont quick-disconnect gas connector was a perfect match. Our product enabled catering operators to mount their gas-cooking equipment on casters. The equipment could then be quickly and easily disconnected from the gas supply and moved away from the wall. This allowed the area to be cleaned, reducing the risk of grease fires and sanitation issues. The benefits of the Dormont concept almost identically mirrored the Mechline product system. Peter and I agreed to work together to tackle the standards challenge. If we could solve this dilemma, Mechline would become our exclusive distributor for the United Kingdom.

I reviewed with Peter the recent history regarding our attempts to gain various types of European certifications, including our CE mark registration and subsequent revocation by the British Standards Institute. We decided to focus our efforts on the UK standard (BS 669: Part 2) for catering (food-service) gas hoses. The goal would be to obtain BSI certification. Our efforts with the US government had created an opening. Since the bilateral trade agreements between the United States and UK were against the concept of design-restrictive standards, the UK government applied pressure on the standards committee to focus on a performance-based standard. The competitive manufacturers tried to create a series of hurdles, but we addressed all of the issues that they raised. The committee amended the performance requirements in the standard, and we finally could reenter the UK market. The Mechline team did an incredible sales job bringing the Dormont catering hose back into the marketplace, and quickly it became the #1 brand again.

China—The New Frontier

We began to see Chinese imports become increasingly prevalent in the plumbing industry. It seemed like more and more pipes, valves, and fittings were being imported from Asia. We were starting to get pricing pressure on our gas ball valves, as the manufacturers from Taiwan and China were expanding from water into gas ball valves. I was also getting inquiries from Chinese companies that claimed that they were manufacturing stainless steel water and gas connectors. We had heard that some of our competitors were buying their fittings from China. We knew that we had to go to China and find out firsthand what was happening. Our future viability in a highly competitive market could be at risk.

One of our biggest concerns about doing business in China was how we could protect our proprietary technology. One incident that reinforced our apprehension occurred when we met with a delegation of Chinese politicians and business-development executives from Tianjin, a city outside of Beijing. They conducted a business presentation that highlighted the advantages of their city as a great place for us to set up a manufacturing location in China. I asked the mayor of the Tianjin about how we could protect our intellectual property, and his answer was illuminating. He said: "Mr. Segal, if we copy your product, it is a sign of great respect. You are the master, and we learn from you as a student. If we do not copy your product, maybe your product is not very good." An interesting cultural explanation to justify intellectual property theft.

In order to gain more knowledge, I attended a Young Presidents Organization (YPO) seminar in California. I had been a YPO member for many years and found it to be an invaluable organization for learning and business knowledge. Several sessions discussed the ways for companies to start working with Chinese manufacturers. As a small-to-mid-sized manufacturer, we did not have the size to hire our own full-time employees to help with potential sourcing options. We uncovered several firms who focused specifically on helping companies like Dormont identify, qualify, and build supplier relationships with Chinese companies.

We met with one of these firms and discussed several areas of interest, including component parts, flexible stainless steel tubing, and gas-connector assemblies. If a Chinese manufacturer was making a stainless steel gas connector that could compete with us, I wanted to see it and learn as much as I could about the firm. On our first trip, I went with our vice president of manufacturing and one of our engineers. The consulting firm had arranged for us to visit fifteen to twenty companies. It promised to be a long, grueling, and challenging trip.

We arrived in Shanghai, where our guide/interpreter met us at the airport, and we discussed our objectives over dinner. Over the next ten days, we saw an amazing range of companies. Some were highly automated and sophisticated; others had a large number of employees who did most tasks by hand. It was a completely different operating environment than in the United States. The average employee earned between fifty cents and one dollar per hour. Almost all employees lived in a factory-provided dormitory, where they were provided with housing and meals. The factories did not have the safety rules and regulations that are required in the United States. We saw employees working with molten metal in a hot forge wearing open-toed sandals and no protective eyeglasses. We observed people kneeling around boxes where they were sorting items and assembly lines where large quantities of products were being manually assembled. One factory owner told me he was building a new five hundred thousand sq. ft. factory. I asked him what he would manufacturer in the facility, and he did not know. He was confident in the growth of his business, and he knew that he would find new business opportunities (and workers) to fill it up. Yes, this is what the Industrial Revolution on steroids must look like.

Our primary concern regarding any products sourced from China was quality. Could the company provide consistently verifiable high-quality products? One way to help ensure quality was to have the consulting firm have one of their engineers inspect the operations on a regular basis. In addition, we could pay for a person to check items from every container before it left the factory. In addition, we could require written certification that the items met our material specifications for every shipment. We had heard horror stories about problems with Chinese products, some of which occurred after a company had been doing business for several years. We knew that we would need to have multiple checks and balances to ensure that we would be comfortable with items purchased from China.

After we returned from our trip, we received a number of quotes from the companies that we had visited. If the prices were indeed accurate, it was clear that we needed to begin to source some items from China to maintain our competitive viability. Our strategy was to slowly introduce certain items into our mix, including fittings and ball valves.

In terms of Chinese gas-connector manufacturers, there were a few companies that had been able to copy our design, but none that had the knowledge or capability yet to manufacture them in large quantities. We knew that one day this could represent a significant threat, especially if a large retailer like Home Depot decided to buy directly from their Shanghai purchasing office. I also visited several manufacturers in order to understand their capabilities. This proved to be an invaluable learning experience. The incremental costs related to shipping, lead times, extra quality control, and potential currency fluctuations provided us with the knowledge that we could effectively compete by further focusing on improving our internal operations and supply-chain opportunities with domestic suppliers.

After we sold Dormont, we began to work closely with a number of Chinese companies that were 100 percent owned by the corporate parent. It was very interesting to learn how they operated when you were able to see the "real numbers"—or at least the numbers that they showed when you were the owner. Even then, we were never quite sure if they were being totally truthful. It seemed to be somewhat of a game, wherein they would be able to meet or provide a cost estimate lower than our target. When we tried to break out the costs, line item by line item, the actual figures got a bit fuzzy, so you weren't always sure if you were making money. In addition, the Chinese government required that we add a 20 percent profit to the actual transfer cost, funds that would have to remain in country. So while a company might be making profits in China, it was unclear if we would ever be able to repatriate them.

Korea

Over the years, I received a number of inquiries from Korean companies that were interested in working with Dormont. As part of our efforts to explore new-product opportunities, we thought it would make sense to visit a few companies in Korea to learn more about their companies and products. As we had learned, it was a good practice to be open-minded and listen to potential suppliers about new business opportunities.

One company that I met with was actively involved in manufacturing corrugated stainless steel tubing for gas and water piping, gas connectors, and flexible sprinkler drop lines. These sprinkler drop lines really piqued our interest. They were utilized in the installation of a fire-protection piping system in commercial buildings. This was a very similar concept to our flexible gas connectors, where a flexible stainless steel assembly could replace hard piping. This type of installation would be much faster, easier, and less expensive because there was no pipe cutting and assembly required. This product has become successful in the North American fire safety market. This was another great example of finding a new product and market because we were willing to explore opportunities in overseas markets.

South America—Example of Country and Market Risks

The size of scope of the South America market makes it of great interest to most companies that export their products. We were selling our foodservice gas connectors through export distributors, who sold them to foodservice equipment distributors throughout the continent. Our challenge was to find a distribution partner for our higher volume residential gas connectors. They needed to understand the requirements and certifications for the various countries and be able to distribute them to plumbing/heating companies.

We were contacted by a Brazilian company that was interested in selling our products in South America. We worked closely with them to develop a detailed market-introduction plan. This included redesigning the end fittings, translating the installation instructions, and revising the packaging to meet their requirements. We worked closely with them and the national gas companies to obtain product approvals in both Brazil and Argentina.

Just as we were about to launch the product line, there was a political/economic crisis in Brazil that led to a significant devaluation in the Brazilian currency. This effectively doubled the delivered cost of our product, making a stainless steel option extremely difficult to sell when compared with domestic rubber-hose options. This currency devaluation hurt many businesses and forced our Brazilian distribution partner to abandon the program.

This reinforced the concept that it is easy to underestimate the complexity, cost, and challenges of overseas markets. A company might be incredibly successful in their local (home-country) market and think that it will be able to easily transfer the same skills and methods to achieve similar results in international markets. It is important that you proceed with caution and carefully understand the business, regulatory, political, and economic risks and costs associated with overseas markets.

Lessons Learned—International Partnerships

1. **Working with international business partners will introduce you to new business, social, and cultural practices that will expand your horizons.**
   We developed strong personal relationships that transcended the business realm. These relationships were rewarding in many ways and provided a window into the lives of our friends overseas. From a business perspective, you can go beyond traditional barriers to develop relationships that will allow you to grow personally and can greatly benefit your company.

2. **International business partners can expand your knowledge through the introduction of new business practices and innovative products.**
   Our relationships created a pathway for us to learn about business concepts (e.g., Toyota Production System, lean manufacturing) and new and advanced technology (production equipment).

3. **International business partners can help you develop your overseas markets.**
   Many of our relationships started out with companies providing us with components for our gas-appliance connectors. As they got to know our company, they became interested in selling our products directly or helping us find in-country distributors.

4. **It may be critical to have an in-country business partner in overseas markets to help fight trade barriers designed to protect local manufacturers.**
   Standards can be used to effectively deny your company access to international markets. This can be a challenging hurdle. We were able to get a seat at the table to influence UK authorities. Our distributor had the technical knowledge to help us fight the standards battle.

5. **The more you learn about international business practices, the more you will realize how little you actually know.**

In every country, there are unique cultural customs and business practices that add complexity and variability to your relationship. It is important to learn as much as you can about these customs and have great respect for them. However, you want to have your guard up to ensure that you are not taken advantage of. As we worked in China, we were never confident that our potential suppliers were being truthful. You weren't sure if you could build a relationship based on quotations, laws, and regulations that could change at any moment. It is important to have systems in place to verify that quality, specification and materials used in your products.

6. **An analysis that compares overseas sourcing with domestic production must look beyond the snapshot numbers.**

It is extremely important to build risk factors into your decision-making process. Factors that you may need to consider include theft of intellectual property, incremental shipping costs, dramatically increased lead times, extra quality control at overseas factories and their suppliers, potential product liability and litigation costs, the impact of currency fluctuations, changes in tax structure, duties, additional fees, the requirement to keep a percentage of the profits in the overseas markets, and labor and environmental regulations.

7. **Do not underestimate the complexity, cost, and challenges of overseas markets.**

When approached by potential distribution partners in South America, we developed a market entry plan. We were poised to implement the plan—and then Brazil and Argentina encountered an economic crisis driven by political instability. You may be successful in domestic markets and think that you will be able to easily transfer the same skills and methods to achieve similar results in international markets. It is important that you proceed with caution and carefully understand the risks and costs associated with all overseas markets.

8. **The best way to understand overseas markets in to learn about them firsthand.**

   There has been a great deal written about the enormous potential and significant threats posed by China and other emerging countries (India, Brazil, etc.). The best way to understand these challenges and opportunities is to attend a trade show, visit potential suppliers and competitors, and see for yourself what your company will encounter in a global market.

9. **You can develop your international sales through relationships with your customers.**

   Many of our gas connectors were used overseas by our multinational customers who used them in their international locations. In addition, export distributors that bundle the products of many manufacturers can provide an excellent avenue to facilitate international business.

Chapter 6
Marketing: Romancing the Hose!

If it sells, it's beautiful.
—Harry Segal

In a business-to-business environment, it can be a challenge to generate excitement about a product. This was particularly true with flexible gas-appliance connectors, which were relegated to the often-boring plumbing category. I knew that we could make our products interesting and energize our distributors. In this chapter, I highlight examples of sales meetings, packaging, and promotions that captured the interest of our target audiences. These were integrated into our overall marketing efforts to build the strength of the Dormont® Brand. The ability to take a gas connector and make it interesting was a concept that I often called "Romancing the Hose!"

Sales Meetings

I have sat through hundreds of sales meetings throughout my career, and most have been incredibly boring. They tend to be the same old "rah-rah," here is our plan, now let's go get 'em. I decided early on that I wanted my sales meetings to be different—to truly be exciting, informative, and yes, even memorable. It is important to keep your sales representatives engaged so that they are attentive and can learn how to effectively sell your products and be excited about representing your company.

My first opportunity came as a brand manager at Scott. Our national sales meeting was being held at the PGA Resort in West Palm Beach. Over five hundred people attended, including our entire field sales and marketing staff. Prior to the meeting, our advertising agency had come up with that year's theme: "Catch the Fire." They had purchased the rights to the song and rewritten the words, hiring a local band to record the new version. We spent a lot of money to create this program, but to me it fell flat. Our wiper business unit was going to lead one of breakout sessions during the meeting. I wanted to think about a creative, inexpensive way that we could attract attention at the meeting. So I began to look for popular songs and movies that would play off of our primary sales concept; that paper-based disposable wipers could replace cloth rags. The movie *Ghostbusters* had been a huge hit that year. Its poster featured a ghost with the universal red circle with a line through the center, implying "no ghosts."

I went to a T-shirt shop and had them make up six shirts that had the word "cloth" with the red circle/line printed over the top—"no cloth." This seemed to be a quick, simple image that would play off of *Ghostbusters* by creating a "Clothbusters" theme. It also captured the main essence of our sales message. We asked the senior managers if they would pose for a few pictures wearing the Clothbusters shirt. We encouraged them to give us their best grimace, as if they were truly fighting against the evil, wicked cloth-shop towels. Needless to say, we had a great time taking the pictures, laughing a lot, and not telling anyone how we planned to use them.

The first night of the meeting, there was a big launch party, but it seemed like most of the folks just wanted to catch up with friends. Another year, another theme, another meeting. The next day there were four breakout sessions. It was time to launch our plan. We had approximately 125 people in a breakout room at 9:00 a.m., all expecting the typical sales meeting format. Many were still sleepy, some were hung over, and all were prepared to be bored to tears. In setting the mood, it is important to know that Bob, our marketing manager, was a very straight-laced, no-nonsense person. So the lights went down, the people settled into their seats—and the *Clothbusters* theme began to play. Then the pictures of the Scott senior leaders were projected onto a screen. And Bob began to sing loudly into the microphone: "You're out on the street, and you're selling against rags—who you going call, Clothbusters! I ain't afraid of no rag!!!"

All of the sudden, people in the audience start to laugh loudly—and began to clap and sing along: "Who you gonna call—Clothbusters!" And then to the amazement of the entire audience, Bob did a moonwalk across the stage. The entire rooms shrieked in laughter! We then proceeded with our presentation, but people were happy and upbeat and actually listening. When our session ended, the people in the other breakout rooms stumbled into their next boring meeting. However, they wanted to know what all the laughing and clapping was about in the wiper meeting. We repeated the session three more times, with each crowd getting louder and more into the song.

Later that day, our business team gathered to discuss how much fun people had and what a super meeting it was. Then our senior vice president came over to me and told me how angry he was. He then said that I had spent twenty dollars on my meeting, while he had spent five hundred thousand dollars with the ad agency—and people liked our theme better. I knew that he was happy for us, but it was also a great lesson. You didn't need to spend a lot of money to generate excitement and to create a fun atmosphere—you just had to have a good idea and be willing to put yourself out there.

At Dormont, I brought the same type of fun to our sales meetings. These were held every two years in conjunction with the National Association of Food Equipment Manufacturers (NAFEM) convention. There were significant differences that made this meeting more of a challenge. First of all, we employed manufacturers' representatives, who were independent sales agencies that represented other manufacturers. Prior to the start of the show, all manufacturers wanted to have a meeting. So we were competing against the other manufacturers to see if we could get our reps to come to a Dormont meeting. We usually had an early breakfast meeting with the hope that we could attract more of our reps due to fewer meeting conflicts.

I decided to build on my successful experience at Scott for the Dormont meeting. The challenge was that while the Dormont gas hose was a valued product, it was not the most exciting topic for a sales meeting. I knew we had to bring some outside ideas to liven up the meetings, like we did with Ghostbusters. I wanted to find an upbeat, catchy song that most people would know the words to. One type of music that generates good feelings is reggae music, as it is often heard when people are on vacation in the islands. One of the most popular songs is "Hot, Hot, Hot," which seemed to have a natural connection to "Hose, Hose, Hose." We went through the meeting, and I told the reps that we had a surprise for them at the end.

We started up the music and passed out a lyrics sheet (so they could sing along), and out came our sales manager, dressed up as a reggae pop star. This was totally new approach and different from all other NAFEM-type meetings. Our reps absolutely loved it. Toward the end of the song, one of the top reps in the country started a conga line. We had the entire room dancing in a conga line at 9:00 in the morning. Wow! The feedback from the meeting was incredible. Other factories wanted to know what we had done. It was certainly a big point of discussion and many laughs during the rest of the show. The question was how we could top it at the next NAFEM meeting. Future show themes played on the Fifties (Blue Hose (Moon), the Village People (Dormont (Macho) Man), Motown (My Hose (Girl)), and Sports Themes. I learned that we could make our sales meetings exciting, something that our reps would look forward to. It also set the stage for us to introduce new products and programs to an audience that was receptive and attentive.

Packaging and Point-of-Sale Displays
As I made sales calls with our reps, I realized that their day-to-day routine could become quite monotonous. They would make regular rounds with the distributors in their territory and integrate end-user calls along the way. Each visit to a distributor involved the obligatory "bringing of the donuts," saying hello to folks in the office and warehouse, and checking in with the purchasing agent. An item like a Dormont gas connector was specified with gas-cooking equipment (often for specific jobs or projects), but it was purchased like a supply item. A simple check of inventory in the warehouse by the purchasing agent would determine if an order needed to be placed. So our challenge was how to make gas connectors interesting to distributors and their salespeople.

Food-Service Distributor Packaging
Early in the product life cycle of Dormont gas connectors, we developed an ingenious idea to get the products out of the warehouse and onto the distributor showroom floor. We developed a point-of-sale (POS) program using a blister-pack (a plastic-sealed cardboard sheet) that would hang on a rack. We encouraged distributors to place these POS racks near the

gas-cooking equipment on the showroom floor. Over a period of years, we continued to upgrade and improve the program. We revised the color scheme, added graphics, and switched to a sturdy pegboard rack. The Dormont POS display rack was a silent salesman on the showroom floor. We encouraged distributor sales people to help their customers (and improve the profitability of the sale) by including a Dormont gas-appliance connector with every piece of gas-cooking equipment that they sold.

We wanted to continue to build on this success, so we explored how our products were being displayed, used, and installed out in the field and made the following observations:

- **Functionality:** There was no way to easily tell what this product did or how it was used unless you were familiar with it. This was an issue for someone not familiar with caster-mounted gas equipment. The Package also needed a handle and a bar-code label.
- **Appearance:** Sometimes the plastic package did not look good—the corners may have been bent in shipping, the plastic may not have adhered properly to the board, the peg-holes may have been damaged, or people may have opened up the plastic to touch the product.

We developed a new four-color gas-connector installation kit, a rectangular box that could be used on existing POS displays. The color graphics showed the product in use—a great picture of a person cleaning behind a gas range with a disconnected gas connector beside him. Since the products were inside the sealed box, a person could not easily pilfer something off the display. We integrated a sturdy plastic handle that made it easy to hang the kit on a POS display or carry it to a truck or an installation location. This new package addressed the previous issues.

The new box design worked extremely well, and we used it as a platform for future line extensions. Our distributors loved the new kit boxes because they were easy to store, display, and ship. There were several unanticipated benefits:

- **Catalog Distributors:** The kits worked well with our catalog distributors, companies that sold a wide array of food-service products that were merchandised in a catalog, because it made it easier to handle and reship the boxes.
- **Service Agencies:** Our service agency customers loved the kits because they were easy to transport to installation sites—and they created a POS opportunity at their parts counter.
- **Trade Shows**: Using empty kit boxes made it easier to set up displays at trade shows. The four-color graphics showed the products, and it was more convenient than shipping products back and forth. They also worked great at tabletop shows and distributor buying conferences.
- **Specification:** We had always worked to get our products specified by architects, kitchen design consultants, and food-service chains. The concept of an "installation kit" was easy and simple to comprehend—and it made it easier to recommend and get our kits specified.

The Dormont POS display-rack program was a huge success. We placed displays in almost every food-service equipment distributor around the country. We referred to these displays as cash machines for our distributors, because every gas connector sold represented additional revenues and profits for them. It also provided great value to the kitchen operators, for it helped to ensure that movable gas connectors were installed safely and properly. This is a great example of how a company can reenergize it sales by taking a product line and integrating an attractive packaging program and POS display for its distributors and end-use customers.

Residential Packaging Programs

As our residential business continued to increase, we began to develop a plan to pursue the retail channel of distribution. We had to develop a packaging program that would meet the display requirements of multiple channels. We pursued two paths to address this opportunity: (1) a private-label program for major appliance manufacturers and (2) a poly-bagged program where we added an innovative twist. Our solution would have to work in various types of stores and merchandising environments.

We analyzed the retail-packaging programs of our competitors and found them to be quite confusing. It was difficult to understand what gas connector should be used with what gas appliance. When we asked employees at retailers for assistance, they were equally confused. We often saw frustrated and angry consumers at the gas-connector section in a home-improvement store ripping open bags to find an end fitting. What was supposed to be a quick job was now taking all afternoon. Our goal was to simplify the program, making it easier for the consumer to select the right product. We also wanted to help retailers increase their profitability.

Building on our experience with food-service gas connectors, we addressed this problem by creating a residential gas-appliance installation kit. Our goal was to reduce the number of SKUs from twelve to two. There would be one for gas ranges and one for gas dryers.

- **Length:** The depth of most gas ranges and dryers is thirty inches. We determined that a forty-eight-inch connector would provide enough room for an installer to attach the connector to the appliance and gas supply and push the appliance back into place. Rather than offer three different sizes, we decided to offer only a forty-eight-inch option.
- **End Fittings:** We determined that if we included an extra fitting, it would address almost all installation options and reduce the number of items. The cost of the fitting was small, and it made life easier for the retailer and the installer.
- **Installation Components:** We also included a small tube of both pipe-thread sealant (in order to make a proper connection) and a noncorrosive leak-detection solution.

We selected a clamshell package, which was a great solution for both Dormont and our customers. Internally, we could use the same shell for both the gas range and gas dryer kits. We would switch the four-color insert label in the front and include the appropriate components in each. We were also able to change the label to switch from a Dormont®-branded product to a private-label product. Once again, we used the same clamshell package for all options. We outsourced the coiling of the connectors and assembly of the insert packages (pipe sealant, leak test solution, instructions) to a

Special-Needs workshop. We were able to make a positive contribution to the community and help our customers.

For our customers, we were able to dramatically reduce the number of gas connector items from twelve to two SKUs. Retailers were able to reduce shelf space, increase inventory turns, and reduce pilferage. Our new kits also represented a higher price point, delivering additional dollars to the bottom line. Retail employees could now help customers with their questions. If a customer was buying a gas range, they would be directed them to the orange kit. If they were buying a gas dryer, they would be told to select a red box. And the homeowner/installer was happy, because all of the items (other than tools) needed to make the connection were there. No more extra trips back to the store. We also developed a separate water-heater installation kit that was sold in the water-heater section.

These private-label kits were sold in multiple channels of distribution, including home-improvement retailers, hardware stores, appliance-parts distributors, and catalog distributors. This was a great example of going back to the basics and listening and watching how your product is purchased, installed, and used in the field. Asking questions and listening to installers and end users will uncover issues and areas of frustration. This will provide you with the information to help design a superior product and/or a packaging solution that may help increase your sales.

Poly-Bagged Program
In order to compete in the plumbing section of the retail channel, we had to develop a poly-bagged packaging program. We analyzed the POP programs of other manufacturers in multiple categories and saw that there were opportunities for improvement. We helped to change this category by introducing color-coded products with improved graphics. Our internal teams utilized our Kaizen processes to improve both the efficiency of our work cells and the effectiveness of the packaging. Each new customer often had special requirements, which added to the complexity of the program. Below are several items that were elements of the programs.

Planogram: We quickly became knowledgeable in the world of planograms, which provided a template for the location of products in a retail space. We would develop customized planograms for each retailer based on their requirements, working with the category manager and usually someone from store operations. Typically, we would set up a prototype planogram in a warehouse or store selected by the retailer. They would examine the display and make additional suggestions.

Color: We were offering three different diameters of gas connectors, so we selected a separate packaging color for each size—orange for ranges, red for dryers, and green for water heaters. This was a first in the gas-connector category. We packaged the fittings in colored bags that corresponded to the appliance and connector.

Bags: We needed to develop a cost efficient was to purchase and seal the plastic bags. Our engineers and employees designed a highly efficient work cell, including a semi-automated machine. The bags were supplied on a roll and there was a heat sealing device that closed the bag after the connector was inside.

When entering a new market opportunity, it is important to examine the transactional experience from the perspective of both the distributor and the consumer. Careful observation and numerous discussions can identify problem areas or sources of frustration. We were able to introduce numerous improvements that made it easier for consumers to select the right gas connector and improved the category profitability for our retail customers.

Distributor Promotional Items

Most companies buy a wide variety of promotional items with imprinted logos. These include pens, mugs, bags, hats, memo pads, and a wide range of related junk. There is an appropriate Yiddish word for this stuff—***dreck***—which means "worthless trashy stuff, especially low-quality merchandise." If we were going to give away stuff, I wanted it to be items that people would keep. Otherwise it was like throwing money away. Some of the most successful items that we used included:

Travel Coffee Mugs—The mugs could be used by people (especially distributor salesmen, equipment installers, plumbers, and service agencies) while they were driving from call to call. Each time they got a cup of coffee, they would see the Dormont name.

Dormont Doughnut Boxes—It is the custom of sales people to bring doughnuts into their first few calls in the morning. They will typically stop at a local shop and pick up a few dozen. These are put out in the kitchenette area near the coffee machine (or at the wholesale counter of a distributor). One issue is that most people who eat the doughnuts don't know who brought them, since the salesman just puts the box down We decided to have doughnut boxes printed with the Dormont name and logo, along with a "thank you" to our customers. This would let people know who brought the doughnuts.

Quick-Disconnect Key Chains—The chains could carry a car key on one end and other keys on the other. This could be disconnected when you had to valet a car or leave the keys at a garage or parking lot. The keychain reminded people of the Dormont quick disconnect gas connector.

Personalized Louisville Slugger Wooden Baseball Bats—Rather than give out wooden plaques that would sit in a closet and collect dust, we liked to reward valuable contributors with a personalized wooden baseball bat. Any kid who grew up playing baseball dreamed of one day being a major league baseball player. One of the benefits of making it to "The Show" is having your own personalized baseball bat. So to receive a bat with your name in script was a sign that you had "made it to the big time." I have visited customers many years after they received their Louisville Slugger—and the bat still has a prominent place in their office.

Phone Swivels—These gizmos could be attached to a phone between the handset and cord, preventing the cord from getting tangled. Each time the person picked up the phone, they would see the Dormont name.

Plush Toys—Before Beanie Babies became popular, I thought that they would make a great leave-behind gift for an administrative assistant, a purchasing agent, or a secretary. These cute beanbag animals would sit on people's desks, a reminder of their friends at Dormont.

Tape Measures—When we introduced the Dormont Supr-Swivel™, one of the selling features was that equipment could be moved closer to the wall, thereby saving inches of aisle space. To emphasize this benefit, we gave out imprinted tape measures. Since this is an item that is often used, the tape measures became a useful tool.

Sculpture Award—As a reward for our top sales reps, we wanted to give them something more memorable and longer lasting than just cash or a plaque. My aunt had created a bronze sculpture of an orchid mounted on a marble base. This beautiful piece of art, with an inscribed plaque, became known and valued by our manufacturers' rep agencies. This was another example of putting thought behind an award to thank valued partners for their help in our mutual success.

When purchasing promotional items for your company, it is important to select items that will stand out. Think about what your customers might really want and provide them with items that will be used and appreciated and that add value to your investment.

Distributor-Reward Programs

We knew that purchasing agents sometimes needed an incentive to place larger orders. It was common in a seasonal business (like plumbing or HVAC wholesale) to offer extended payment terms as an incentive for a distributor to place a larger than normal order. In a competitive business environment, the buyer had become accustomed to this type of offer. The payment terms were often extended to forty-five, sixty, or even ninety days. In addition, purchasing agents were often offered more attractive payment terms for preseason orders. Theoretically, this compensated the distributor for the time value of money, but in reality, it also was an attempt to load up a distributor's inventory (thereby locking out competition).

The question for us was how could we design a program with extended payment terms (dating) and increased prepayment discounts that stood out from others. We knew that purchasing agents liked to receive gifts, as long as they weren't too valuable or didn't seem to indicate some type of improper behavior. We began to experiment with a program that would offer a prize (of increasing value) based on order size, along with extended dating and more attractive payment terms. We started the program during the baseball season and patterned it using four levels:

Level I	Buy 250 gas hoses, 2.5 percent 30, net 31 days
Level II	Buy 500 gas hoses, 3.0 percent 30, net 31 days
Level III	Buy 750 gas hoses, 3.5 percent 60, net 61 days
Level IV	Buy 1000 gas hoses, 4.0 percent 60, net 61 days

The prizes were targeted at 1 percent of the order value, or roughly $10 for Level I, $20 for Level II, $30 for Level III, and $40 for Level IV. We would develop a theme for the program and then select "rewards" that purchasing agents would want. These included sports-related merchandise and memorabilia, Bass Pro catalog items, holiday gifts for children, and backyard BBQ tools, just to name a few. We even included programs for Mother's Day and Valentine's Day, where a purchasing agent could have flowers sent to their spouse just by placing an order.

Reward programs, if executed well, are a great way to change a boring stocking program into an exciting activity. These programs were highly valued and greatly appreciated by both our distributors and our reps. Dormont was making selling fun again. They could make calls on their distribution customers and offer them a nice gift in appreciation for their order. The program became very popular, and purchasing agents began to look forward to sales call from Dormont reps, as they wanted to know what we had come up with next.

Holiday Cards/Gifts

Another opportunity to differentiate our business was through our holiday cards and gifts. We always tried to create programs that were unique and memorable and provided some value and/or appreciation with our business partners and key customers. Every holiday season a large volume of seasons' greetings cards would inundate us. One after another they came, and they were often placed around the lunchroom and then eventually discarded after the start of the New Year. Rarely was there any distinguishing factor. It just seemed like an expense that yielded little return. It was expected but not valued.

I had seen an adorable card with two young girls, and an idea flashed into my head. Wouldn't it be nice to incorporate my daughters into a customer-appreciation card? But instead of sending them when everyone did, it seemed that Valentine's Day would be a great opportunity. We could tell our customers how much we appreciated their business and how we loved working with them.

This idea transformed into a series of Valentine's Day cards featuring my daughters in an interesting theme or vignette. These were all developed and orchestrated by my wife—and our daughters were great sports. The themes included Alice in Wonderland, the 60s, ice-skating, and holding hearts. Our customers "loved" the cards—and they became a February highlight. In fact, as I would travel around the country in a number of offices I saw the cards from different years sequentially affixed to the wall. This was a great example of taking something that is a given and turning it into a creative program that can better connect your customers to the company. What message is better than telling your customers that you love them?

We also had a small program of holiday gifts for our largest customers. Once again, I wanted the gift to be something useful that would be appreciated and valued by our customers. I enlisted the help of my wife (Tracy) and my administrative assistant (Theresa) in thinking up fun gifts every year. We often selected gifts for the home kitchen, a place where families gather and where a well-thought-out gift would be used over and over again. We would select the items and package them in an attractive straw basket. Some of the more memorable gifts included a bagel slicer and spreading knives; a redwood outdoor BBQ set; a beautiful holiday carving set; and a set of garden tools and gardening gloves. These holiday gift baskets were highly appreciated, for people knew the thought and effort that went into creating a special holiday thank you.

Lessons Learned—Marketing: Romancing the Hose!

1. **Creating a fun environment for sales meetings can create a better opportunity to convey your message.**
    In an effort to break through the noise and boredom of traditional sales meetings, we developed a concept that made our meeting the "one to attend." Our reps always wanted to see what we had come up with next. This provided us with a platform where they were interested and excited to learn about our new products and services

2. **Effective, eye-catching packaging can have a major impact on sales.**
    Packaging can affect how a product is perceived and can provide a quick tutorial on how and where an end user can utilize your product. Four-color graphics and a functional package design can help increase your sales.

3. **Listen to end users' comments about how they purchase and use your products.**
    In order to develop the new packaging, we listened to our end users and watched how our products were purchased, installed, and used in the field. This process can uncover issues and areas of frustration. This will provide you with the information to help design a superior product and/or a packaging solution. We were able to improve our packaging, reduce the number of SKUs, and increase our customers' profitability and inventory turns.

4. **Look for opportunities to work with special-needs workshops.**
    With the full support of our employees, we worked with a special-needs workshop to meet some of our retail packaging requirements. We were able to support a noble effort and provide meaningful work that benefitted our local community.

5. **Distributor rewards programs can build loyalty and generate excitement.**

   Our rewards programs were highly valued and greatly appreciated by our reps and our customers. We made selling fun again. They could then make calls on their distribution customers and offer them a nice gift in appreciation for their order. Purchasing agents began to look forward to sales call from Dormont reps, as they wanted to know what we had come up with next.

6. **Creative ideas can make customer interactions unique, special, and memorable.**

   We were able to take a holiday card and turn it into a creative program that allowed us to emotionally connect our customers to the company. What better message than to tell your customers that you love them!

7. **Provide promotional items that add value rather than end up in a landfill.**

   We carefully thought about the promotional items that we offered and asked a simple question: Is this something that I really want? We looked for promotional items that stood out when compared with the typical array of dreck that most companies put out.

Chapter 7
Customers

Make your product easier to buy than your competition,
Or you will find your customers buying from them, not you.
—Mark Cuban

We had the opportunity to work with a wide range of customers in many different channels of distribution. They ranged from wholesale distributors to large retail chains to equipment manufacturers. Each channel and every customer was unique, and these differences created the opportunity to learn and build programs and services that would create value for our customers. The competitive dynamics in each of our business units were very different, which always made life interesting. We also had the ability to take the knowledge and successes that we developed in one channel and apply that learning to customers in other channels of distribution. Our goal was to build a strong relationship with our customers, one that they would hold out as a model to their other suppliers. I knew that we had reached a goal when a customer would say, "I wish all of my suppliers were like Dormont."

Large Retail Customers
Working with large retail customers can present a business with both significant opportunities and risks. The scope of activities and support required can be a mystery. The first step is to examine your own company in terms of what these retailing giants are looking for in a supplier:

1. **Strong brand recognition/consumer pull-through**: They want a brand that sells itself, one that their customers will recognize when they see it on the shelf. If the manufacturer advertises the product,

the retailer will benefit because they capitalize on the pull-through effect. This was a challenge for Dormont as we had established our position in the wholesale, business-to-business marketplace. One way that we addressed this objective was through a private-label program with General Electric. The GE brand was globally known, and our GE-branded products sold well in the installation accessory area of an appliance department.

2. **Meet/exceed margin targets:** The retailer wants products that meet/exceed their financial target for profitability and inventory turns. Our ability to achieve continuous improvement in our manufacturing operations allowed us to profitably sell to the large retailers at a price that met their needs.

3. **Attractive packaging:** The retailer wants a colorful, attractive, and informative planogram that draws the attention of consumers and helps to stimulate purchases. Where appropriate, they want packaging that makes it easy for the customer to make the right purchasing decision, thereby reducing returns. Through our packaging innovations, we were able to increase inventory turns, reduce the number of items, and provide a color-coded system that made selection easier for consumers.

4. **In-store service:** Many retailers want manufacturers that will provide in-store service to make sure that the planograms are stocked and look good. Theoretically, this is the job of the retailer's inventory folks, but they have found a way to outsource it to the suppliers. Some retailers have also moved to reducing the number of companies that are allowed to provide in-store service for planograms. In order to address this requirement, we worked with in-store service companies that were approved by the retailers.

5. **China pricing:** Retailers want the most competitive price available. They sometimes use the phrase "China pricing," meaning that they want all suppliers to offer a price that is competitive with the best available price that could be found from a low-cost company in China. While there are a significant number of extra costs associated with doing business in China (quality, availability, technical support, legal liability), they often choose to ignore these and look only at the invoice price. We made numerous trips to China so that we could understand the potential threat from Chinese manufacturers. We aggressively worked to lower our

costs so that we could be competitive and maintain a service and supply-chain advantage.

6. **Vendor consolidation**: Retailers are constantly looking to streamline their operations, lower operating costs, and improve efficiency. One solution is to reduce the number of suppliers, especially if an incumbent can offer additional items. This makes the life of the buyer easier. It also makes it very difficult to dislodge incumbent suppliers. Buyers will use new companies to leverage existing suppliers with no intent of going through the extra work required to change vendors. This proved to be an extremely difficult challenge for our business. Our primary gas-connector competitor sold a full line of residential plumbing products that would take up twenty to thirty feet in a plumbing aisle compared with a three-foot gas-connector section. Our options were to develop private-label customers and focus on the appliance departments.

7. **Stream of new products**: The retailer would like to continue to see new innovative products that will attract customers to their stores. These stimulate traffic and increase sales. Our NPD team aggressively and continuously looked at numerous options to upgrade the gas-connector category.

The Pricing Waterfall

I was amazed at the countless ways that a retailer could ask for additional financial considerations. This is sometimes referred to as the "pricing waterfall," a way for retailer to capture an additional 15-30 percent beyond the invoice price (see appendix). Many organizations are not set up to capture all of these costs to provide a true picture of customer profitability. Their information systems may capture the manufacturing cost of a product, but they do not allocate a full range of marketing and sales-related costs directly to specific customers. The failure to carefully think through and understand the bottom-line impact can impact the financial viability of your company. Below is an extensive list of possible items that you may need to consider in evaluating the economics of doing business with a large retail-chain customer. It may seem long, but each item could be very costly to your business:

1. **Signed vendor-buying agreement (VBA):** This is an extensive, detailed, and one-sided legal agreement drafted by the legal team

of the retailer. It provides them with countless remedies against your company, including hold harmless and indemnification clauses, forcing you to pay all of their legal costs in case of any litigation. Depending on the size of your company, you may not have much leeway in negotiating any changes.

2. **Extremely competitive invoice price:** The retailer wants the lowest invoice price available anywhere in the world, often called the China price. They will selectively ignore many of the important benefits that you offer as a trusted, domestic supplier.

3. **IT set-up/support (EDI, RFID):** There may be a significant investment that is required to meet the electronic business requirements of the retailer. These may include working with their provider of electronic data interchange (EDI) so that you can electronically receive orders and send back confirmations; incorporating into your packaging their unique product numbers and radio frequency identification (RFID) tags; and providing detailed information of package sizes, cubes, and weights that must be provided electronically in the format they request.

4. **Rebate program:** This type of program provides money back to the retailer at the end of the year based on the level of purchases. The retailer would like this be paid in cash but may be willing to accept credit toward future purchases. Buyers are extremely proud about the additional funds that they can recoup from vendors, demonstrating their ability to contribute to the profitability of the company.

5. **New-store opening allowance/slotting fees:** The retailer would like additional discounts and extended payment terms for products purchased for a new store. In some cases, they may ask for free product for the new store as a sign of your mutual investment in the future success of a new location. They will tell you this is all new incremental business. In the grocery industry, suppliers are often required to pay slotting fees, cash payments for preferential shelf placement.

6. **Buy-back allowance:** If you are able to secure a portion or all of a retailer's business, they may require you to "buy back" all of your competitor's products that they have in inventory (stores and warehouse) at the price that they paid, even if it is higher than your price. You must accept the count and dollar amount that they

tell you they shipped to you. (You can sometimes negotiate a cap amount.) And then you are stuck with a significant amount of miscellaneous inventory that is tossed into large cardboard boxes and sent to your factory. Some of the bags are torn and opened with products from other categories thrown in for no reason. You may find someone willing to take these off of your hands, typically at about 10 percent of the amount you gave to the retailer in credit.

7. **Freight prepaid—shipped to individual stores:** Some retailers may ask you to ship small quantities directly to their stores; other may have you send larger shipments to a regional distribution center. These shipments are typically prepaid, meaning that you absorb the cost of shipping. This means that all of your costs increase based on the number, size, and destination of orders that you receive. You can negotiate a minimum order size.

8. **Advertising/co-op allowance:** They may ask for an advertising allowance to support their national and regional advertising efforts. This is typically somewhere between 1 and 3 percent. They may ask for additional money if they want to feature your products in their advertisements.

9. **Support of corporate events/charities:** They may ask you to make a financial commitment to their favorite charities. They may also have a golf tournament, where you can pay an additional $10,000 to ride in a golf cart with your buyer.

10. **Scrap-in-field allowance:** They assume that a certain percentage of your product may be defective. By their definition, "defective" includes packages that are opened by consumers in the store and all returned merchandise. Rather than keeping track of the return and asking for a credit on each one, they negotiate a percentage of their purchases as a discount for what they refer to as "scrap in field." As an aside, a number of companies have developed a profitable business in "reverse distribution," where they take all of the returns from retailers and find a way to sell them, providing the retailer with a commission on the sale.

11. **New signage, store resets:** The retailer may decide to refresh the look of their stores and ask you to provide new signs and update your planograms, at your cost, to improve the appearance of their stores.

12. **Fines for late shipments**: In the VBA, retailers may include a clause that allows them to fine you for late shipments. They typically provide a window (two days) based on the date on the order that they want the product to arrive at their store. If it is in a different UPS delivery zone, you need to adjust to hit their date. Our customer-service people took great pride in meeting the dates and actively investigated every late shipment. Typically, we found them to be caused by human or computer errors of the retailer and had the fines reversed.

13. **Central billing allowance**: Some retailers will offer you the option of sending one invoice rather than individual invoices to each of their stores. They want a fee for this service, which they call a central billing allowance. They know that it saves time and money, and they want a piece of those savings.

14. **Payment terms**: They will negotiate a discount (typically 1-2 percent) and will seek to extend the terms, often to sixty or ninety days. This will allow them work on your money—for they can sell your product and collect revenue from the consumer before they have paid you.

15. **Show discounts**: The hardware store chains often have seasonal (spring and fall) buying shows, where the owners of the franchised stores come to meet with the suppliers. The buyer will negotiate a discount for all orders placed at the show, and they often focus on deals for new products.

16. **Catalog/website pages:** Companies that utilize a catalog (printed, CDs, and online) will ask for a discount or percentage fee to pay for the catalog. The amount is based on the number of pages that they allow you to have in their catalog. They will also ask for financial support for their website, online advertising, and social media efforts.

17. **Preseason allowance**: Retailers and some wholesalers look to increase their inventory levels in anticipation of purchases for seasonal products. They ask suppliers to offer an additional discount in consideration for the increased order size.

18. **In-store service or service agency allowance**: Retailers ask that suppliers hire an agency that will provide in-store service to ensure that all displays look nice, that planograms are stocked, and that all signage and displays are correct. In order to reduce the number of

service agencies, some retailers have required suppliers to select an in-store service company from a list of approved companies. The service agencies typically require a 2-3 percent fee.

19. **Internal costs to support retail customers**: There is a wide range of internal costs that are associated with the support of your retail customers, as their requirements will touch every functional area of your business. From customer service, IT, shipping, and packaging to marketing and sales, you will incur incremental costs based on the requirements of each retailer. You may have to hire additional people and increase your overhead, which may be risky if the retailer changes suppliers.

It is critically important to understand the potential impact of all of these costs when deciding whether or not to do business with a large retail customer. The failure to account for all of these costs can result in significant financial losses for your business.

Home Depot Line Review

For many years, we had been working to secure a portion of the gas-connector business of Home Depot (HD). They had been splitting their purchases between two competitors. One day we received a letter that one of our competitors, an HD supplier, was exiting the gas-connector business. This was a significant change in the competitive dynamics of the gas-connector market. This meant that their customers needed to find a new supplier. Many of them did not like the Goliath in the market, so this represented a great opportunity. The largest customer in this situation was HD.

Shortly after the announcement, we received a phone call from the HD plumbing category manager who invited us to participate in their Annual Line Review. This was a five-day event where they would invite companies in to make a presentation to their buyers for each category. This was an important, often critical, day in the life of a business. For those companies for whom Home Depot represented a large percentage of their sales, the decisions of the buyers could make or break their businesses. We heard stories about people who left the line-review meetings in tears, knowing that the loss of the HD business meant that the future of their company was in jeopardy.

As a first step in the process, the plumbing category buyer asked to visit our factory. Once he arrived, he signed our confidentiality and nondisclosure agreement, a mandatory requirement for all visitors. We wanted the buyer (as we did with every invited guest) to know that we valued and protected our proprietary technology. We went on a factory tour, where we emphasized our ability to effectively handle any or all of HD's gas-connector business. We then went back to the conference room to discuss the upcoming line review. The buyer told us that he was impressed with our facility and was pleased that we would be able to fill the void. He also stated that it was a company policy to not award 100 percent of the business to any manufacturer that produced in one location. They always wanted to have an approved second source just in case there was ever a problem with the primary supplier. We took this as a clear sign that we would be awarded a portion of the HD gas-connector business.

We worked together to prepare a detailed program proposal that include the wide array of topics that need to be addressed with a large retail buyer. At the line review, we provided a number of innovative ideas to complement our overall presentation. We felt confident that we would at least capture a small portion of the business. The plumbing category head buyer had as much told us this when he visited our factory. Our competitor was part of a large corporation that had over five billion dollars in sales with HD. This was truly David vs. Goliath. They were the incumbent, the company that had a history with HD and the big pockets of their corporate parent. In the late afternoon, the head buyer brought us back to the area where the plumbing category team had been deliberating. They told us that they had decided to award 100 percent of the business to Goliath. This was after they had told us about their corporate policy about one-location single source suppliers. Clearly we had underestimated the depth of the deep pockets of our competitor.

This was an incredible learning experience that taught me many lessons, including:

- Never take anything for granted: We believed the head buyer when he said that they had a corporate policy not to single-source a category from a supplier with one manufacturing location. This turned out to be a convenient guideline for them to use as needed rather than a corporate policy.

- It is hard to beat Goliath, but don't forget that you are David. Our competitor was so intent on capturing 100 percent of the HD gas-connector business and they were willing to pay a steep price. We decided to use the results of the HD line review to our advantage. Shortly afterward we approached Lowe's, who was HD's largest competitor. Clearly our competitor and their parent company were deeply rooted with HD. This opened the door for us at Lowe's.

Electronic Auctions

One new trend that presented a significant learning curve was the implementation of "electronic auctions" by one of our largest customers. We were somewhat familiar with the process, as one of the first companies to create this market, Free Markets, was located in Pittsburgh. Several years earlier I had hosted a YPO event that presented a Harvard Business School case study about electronic auctions. The discussion was led by Harvard Professor Benjamin Shapiro and followed by a question and answer session with Free Markets founder.

For each of these auctions, interested companies would receive a package of drawings. There could be several hundred drawings in a bid package, each of which took engineering and sales time to evaluate and to know the range where you could bid. There was a significant amount of gamesmanship in this process, as you saw items where you were the current supplier (a potential loss of volume and/or margin) and new items supplied by your competitors (new sales and profit opportunity).

Our team diligently organized their efforts and prepared themselves for the auction. We ran through a set of scenarios and worked with a consultant to prepare for the event. The day of the auction was stressful, fast-moving, and challenging. At the end, we had won the auction by offering the customer the lowest overall prices. However, it turned out that this was not where the story ended. The customer decided to use the auction bids as a tool to negotiate with its current suppliers. They gave their supplier an ultimatum—meet the lower bid or lose the business. They knew it was easier to stay with an incumbent supplier than to have to go through the effort to qualify and approve a new vendor. This reinforced the lesson about the high-cost barriers to entry for a new supplier.

So while we thought we had won the auction, it turned out that the customer had used us in order to drive their prices lower. In addition, we lost our investment in all of the time required to prepare and develop our quotations. We certainly felt that this violated the intent of the auction process. At that point, we made a strategic decision to slowly back away from that customer. If they wanted to use and spit out suppliers and were not willing to work collaboratively based on mutual trust and respect, they were not the type of customer that we wanted to have as an important part of our business.

Los Angeles Earthquake

We received a phone call from one of our competitors in the gas-connector business. Their largest customer, Sears, was in desperate need of flexible gas connectors as a result of an earthquake in Los Angeles. This presented us with an interesting dilemma. On the one hand, there were people in need in California, and we were in a position to help them. On the other hand, we would be helping out a competitor. Should we say no and hope that Sears would bypass the competitor and come directly to us? If we agreed to help the competitor, would it lead to additional business in the future? What impact would this have on our core business? These were all great questions. However, we stayed true to our values as a company and as a leader. There were people in need, and helping them was the right thing to do.

The challenge was both straightforward and daunting. They needed one hundred thousand gas connectors to be manufactured and transported to Los Angeles as quickly as possible. So we gathered our leadership group together and discussed what actions we would need to take to tackle this challenge. We had to call our major suppliers and find out how quickly they could supply us with the additional inventory needed. We explained the situation and asked for their help in meeting this extraordinary spike in demand. Our team figured out how much inventory we had on hand, the additional amount that we would need to fill the order, and the quantities required to restock our inventory.

We determined that we would need to run our factory at 100 percent capacity 24/7 for at least a week to accomplish this task. We would need additional manpower to make this happen. We met with all of our employees, and everyone agreed to work extended shifts. All of the people who worked in the front office agreed to work in the factory over the weekend. I specifically chose to work the midnight shift on Friday, Saturday, and Sunday in order to demonstrate leadership by my actions. I had always told our employees that I would never ask them to do any job that I had not done.

I remember working on the assembly line at 4:00 a.m. with people from our accounting, customer service, and sales team joining our hourly employees in an all-hands-on-deck effort to meet this challenge. This was a tremendous team effort, and much to the surprise and happiness of Sears and our competitor, we were able to ship the hundred thousand units, in several truckloads, over the course of the next week.

In hindsight, this was a great team-building and bonding experience, one that further helped bring together all of our employees. There were also two interesting twists of fate. A few years later, the competitor decided to drop their brass gas-connector product line and switch to stainless steel. Building on our success from this event, they came to Dormont and we worked out a private-label supply agreement. A second even larger opportunity came when we were able to capture the Sears business. An important part of establishing credibility with Sears was our performance in a time of crisis, along with our OEM relationship with their largest manufacturer of appliances.

Lessons Learned—Customers

1. **The pricing waterfall in an important concept to understand to ensure that you can sustain your profitability.**

   Many organizations are not set up to capture all of the costs that a customer demands in terms of additional discounts and allowances. These can often add up to 15-30 percent beyond the invoice price, a level that can make doing business with certain customers unprofitable. The failure to carefully think through the pricing waterfall and understand the bottom-line impact can impact the financial viability of your company.

2. **A tough business challenge can create an opportunity to bring your team together.**

   Several times we were faced with situations where our customers needed an extraordinary effort. We found that if we brought our people together and explained the challenge, we were able to surmount the issues and eventually solve the problem. Whether it was working 24/7 or driving through the night to deliver products to a customer in need, our team would join together to create an opportunity for our company to shine. We wanted to build on our heritage of always coming through for our customers.

3. **Business challenges may set the table for future opportunities.**

   When we agreed to help our competitor meet their urgent need for Sears, we did not know that it would lay the groundwork for us to eventually work out a private-label supply agreement and later on secure the Sears business. We always tried to do the right thing and build a reputation that others in the industry would respect and value. We often had people whom we worked with call us when they joined a new company, wanting to introduce us to their new employer. Your reputation and how you solve problems will be remembered and valued—and may open new doors for your business.

4. **Never take anything for granted.**

As we found out during the Home Depot line review, people may make comments that are not what they appear to be. We heard a statement that they had a corporate policy not to single-source a category from a supplier with one manufacturing location. This turned out to be a convenient guideline for them to use as needed rather than a corporate policy. An important lesson was reinforced that day: we had to work hard every day to earn the opportunity to work with our customers.

5. **It is hard to beat Goliath, but don't forget that you are David.**

A lesson that was reinforced many times was that a very large competitor might spend a lot of money to hurt your business. In the HD example, they were intent on capturing 100 percent of the gas-connector business, and they were willing to pay the price. We decided to use our slingshot, using the results of the HD line review to our advantage. We approached Lowe's and discussed the lengths that our competitor went to in order to demonstrate their loyalty to Lowe's competitor. Working smarter can sometimes overcome the deep pockets of a competitor.

Chapter 8
Supply-Chain Management

Organizations increasingly find that they must rely on effective supply chains to successfully compete in the global market and networked economy.
—Baziotopoulos

An important element in our success was our ability to work collaboratively with our customers and suppliers. The management of a network of interconnected businesses involved in providing products and services required by end customers is often referred to as supply-chain management (SCM). SCM includes the movement and storage of all raw materials, work-in-process inventory, and finished goods from point of origin to point of consumption. We worked to build a network that developed innovative solutions and leveraged the capabilities of the supply-chain participants.

Competitive Advantage
Our ability to be effective at SCM provided us with several significant competitive advantages. We defined these competitive advantages so that we could clearly communicate to our supply chain partners the value that Dormont brought to the table. One important tool that we used was "Voice of the Customer", which provided invaluable insights regarding customers' needs and requirements. Here are the four key areas where we built our competitive advantage:

- **Time to market of new or modified products and applications**
  We were able to reduce the time required to design, develop, and manufacture products for our customers. The ability to quickly solve customer problems provides significant economic value, for it

delivered reduced costs and greater total savings for our customers. This had a positive impact on their bottom line.

- **Easy to do business with during all customer interactions**

  We worked diligently to improve and upgrade all of our administrative processes. We wanted to ensure that our customers had a great experience with Dormont, and that meant that every "touch" had to be right all of the time. Each step along the path of order fulfillment—taking the order, building the products, shipping the right products, invoicing correctly—had to be done flawlessly. We did not want to develop a great solution and then ruin the experience with the customer due to poor execution.

- **Provide solutions with superior value**

  Our goal was to develop value-added solutions that would deliver financial benefits for our customers. We strived to be creative, thoughtful, and innovative as we searched for ideas that would demonstrate to our customers that we could help enhance their financial performance.

- **Proactive extension of customers' design and manufacturing processes**

  Many of our customers had experienced downsizing that had reduced their purchasing, engineering, and manufacturing staffs. They were extremely busy just keeping the current operation going and had little if any time for new ideas. Our goal was to serve as an "extension" of their team. We worked to become a trusted partner that they could rely on to execute the fundamentals well and then bring suggestions on ways to improve business processes, lower costs, and provide superior solutions.

SCM Processes

It is useful to provide a quick summary of our experiences related to the key SCM processes:

(1) Customer-Service Management

We took great pride in developing close relationships with our customers, trying to understand their buying patterns and going to great lengths to help them out of a jam. Our customer-service team always did a great job at thoughtfully listening to our customers and working with everyone throughout the company to surpass their expectations. For a number of customers, we would proactively call them if they hadn't placed an order recently (based on their historical purchases). They may have forgotten or were busy with other tasks and were greatly appreciative of our support. Most importantly, our high-quality, efficient, and responsive team could turn around orders quickly, usually with products shipping within twenty-four hours after the receipt of an order.

(2) Procurement

A critical component to our success was our outstanding relationship with our stainless steel supplier. As our market share increased, our demand for stainless steel continued to increase at a significant pace. We also continued to upgrade and improve the proprietary equipment that produced our flexible stainless steel tubing. Each of these factors presented opportunities for us to increase our collaboration to improve our supply-chain efficiencies.

From a quality standpoint, we needed a supply partner that could meet all of our technical requirements. An important element was to ensure that the stainless steel was compatible with our proprietary manufacturing process. We worked with our supplier to ensure that the folks at their operations took great care to ensure that the coils were slit, packed, and delivered to meet the stringent requirements of our process. Over time we moved from placing blanket purchase orders to negotiating annual supply agreements. Some of the items that we addressed in the agreement included:

- **Base Price**: We would agree upon a base price for the stainless steel based on the estimated annual tonnage. We had become one of their largest customers, and that usually provided us with some negotiating room.
- **Surcharge**: Given the significant fluctuations in the price for titanium and nickel (materials used in the production of stainless steel), we would receive a formula that would determine the monthly surcharge that would be added to the base price. This surcharge was usually tied to the prices for titanium and nickel on the London Metal Exchange.
- **Annual demand forecast**: We would provide an estimate of our annual demand broken out by the different widths of stainless steel strip based on our historical performance and our projected growth for the upcoming year.

- **Quality**: A material certification was provided with every shipment. If there were any quality issues, their technical folks would quickly come to our factory to review, discuss, and quickly resolve any issues. This was extremely important due to the high inventory turnover that we achieved with their products.

(3) Product Development and Commercialization

One of our important product-development successes involved a collaborative effort between a leading manufacturer of gas-cooking equipment and a multinational food-service chain. By better understanding how our products worked together in their kitchen, we were able to develop an innovative solution. We analyzed the traditional installation of a movable gas connector and noted that gas inlet pipe was located on the backside of the equipment. It made sense for the equipment manufacturer to locate the gas inlet in the rear of the equipment, close to the gas supply line. This made it easier to connect the hard pipe to the gas supply at the wall. The only way to disconnect a movable gas connector was to pull the caster-mounted equipment away from the wall far enough so that a person could reach the quick-disconnect coupling. This meant that the gas hose had to be long enough so that when it was extended, it would allow a person to reach the quick disconnect. Since most gas equipment had been designed with a thirty-six-inch depth, the most common hose length was forty-eight inches. This provided the extra twelve inches of length that was required. Although this was the commonly accepted installation, we thought that there might be a better way.

We were excited about this opportunity because we had always taken as a given the location of the gas inlet of the equipment. The opportunity to work with the engineering teams of the manufacturer and the chain opened up new design opportunities. They thought that it would be great if the design would allow the gas line to be accessed from the front panel of the equipment. This would enable a person to disconnect the gas line before it was moved away from the wall. It also meant that the gas connector could be designed with a shorter length, since it did not need the extra length needed in a traditional installation. We knew that we could design a gas-connector assembly to meet these requirements, but it required the manufacturer to redesign the internal configuration of their equipment. Given the size of the multinational food-service chain, they agreed to these changes.

The design program resulted in a totally new gas-connector configuration. We designed a work cell to assemble all of these components into one complete assembly. We then shipped these assemblies directly to the fryer manufacturer. They then packaged a gas-connector assembly, along with detailed installation instruction, with every gas fryer that was shipped to one of the chain's restaurant locations anywhere in the world.

This was a great example of how new solutions can be developed when multiple partners in the supply chain work collaboratively to address a problem. We took off the constraints of the traditional installation and developed an innovative solution. This strengthened the position of our company and the gas-fryer manufacturer as trusted and valued partners with the multinational chain customer.

(4) Manufacturing Flow Management

We had to continually work with our suppliers to ensure that we could best align our ever-changing customer-demand requirements with their manufacturing schedules. Several techniques that we employed included (a) using a Kanban system, agreeing on the amount of inventory that our key suppliers would keep in reserve at their factory or distribution center. The Kanban system would help determine when and how much inventory we would need and then communicate that on a weekly (or more frequent if needed) basis; (b) working with our suppliers to set up deliveries as frequently as it made economic sense. This was aligned with our goal to maximize our inventory turns and minimize our raw and work-in-process inventory.

(5) Physical Distribution

We worked closely with UPS to manage the increasing amount of shipments as our business continued to grow. We went from one to two to three trucks, eventually moving to a trailer. We managed our order-fulfillment schedule to quickly complete orders and have them ready to go by the end of the first shift. We arranged with UPS to bring the trailer to our facility at approximately 4:00 each day, and we worked together to quickly load up the boxes. In addition, we sometimes received phone calls from distributors who needed gas connectors ASAP or a restaurant would not be able to open. We would find a way to get the products to them, having a rep or someone we knew drop them off at the restaurant. I personally made several deliveries to distributors in the Pittsburgh area on my way home from work.

(6) Performance Measurement

We implemented a certified-supplier program, based upon the needs and requirements of our business, especially as it related to our ISO 9000 certification. In addition, we tried to learn from and draw upon the best practices that we observed in similar programs that we participated in with our customers. Our goal was to improve the quality, delivery, and performance of our suppliers. We developed a supplier scorecard that captured key metrics that we developed in collaboration with our suppliers. The results were compiled and reviewed with our suppliers on a regular basis, and they provided an important means of communicating performance based on actual operating data.

A good example of realized cost reductions was through our incoming inventory inspections. With regular shipments, all incoming goods had to be counted and inspected prior to acceptance. Based on the size of the shipment, this required time of both inventory control and quality-management folks. For those suppliers with a proven record of performance, we could utilize skip-lot inspections, based on the trust and reliability built from a track record of accurate and high-quality deliveries. Working with suppliers who had consistently good quality and correct shipment saved time and money,

Managing Alliance Relationships for Success

It is extremely important to work collaboratively with your suppliers and make them a partner in your success. If they can clearly see the possibility of increased sales, innovative products, and new markets, they will be willing to invest with you to meet your customers' needs. There are numerous benefits that can be realized by developing and managing an effective supply chain. Here are a few examples:

- **Respond quickly to customer demands with more competitive value propositions.**

As you learn more about you customers' operations and the capabilities of your suppliers, you will be able to introduce new ways to rapidly provide solutions. In addition, you will begin to utilize your accumulated knowledge base to offer similar solutions to other customers.

• **Reduce costs and increase profit margins.**

As you learn to apply new methods and processes, you will be able to lower costs within the supply chain and share those with your customers. Being able to solve a problem and save money for a customer is a double win.

• **Focus on your core competencies while relying on supply-chain partners to perform other activities.**

Supply-chain partners have skills sets that have enabled them to build successful businesses. The ability to collaborate and leverage their resources, allowing both you and your suppliers to do what you do best, will enable you to respond faster and more effectively. It will also save you from having to invest in a capability that one of your suppliers already has.

• **Align your company with strong channel partners that will help ensure future competitive success.**

The ability to work with best-in-class suppliers will bring ongoing benefits to your business. These partners can introduce your company to new ideas, products, and technologies that add significant value to your business.

• **Spread risk across the value chain.**

Collaboration with suppliers to offer solutions to your customers will lower your risk, because they become a partner in your joint success. They may be willing to bear some of the costs associated with design, prototyping, and certification, particularly if it creates additional growth opportunities for them. This will reduce your risk by lowering your investment cost.

Selecting Alliance Partners

As we began to focus on SCM, we tried to be thoughtful about where we would spend our time and energy. We wanted to partner with those companies that would align with our strategic goals. We used the following criteria to identify those alliance partners:

- **Highest volume (in purchased $) from the supplier:** Was this one of our largest and most critical suppliers? There were several categories that made up most of the total dollars that we purchased.
- **We represented a significant share of the supplier's business:** This was a mixed bag; on the one hand, it provided us with significant leverage, while on the other hand they might become overly dependent on our company.
- **Unique skills or technology:** If the supplier possesses skills and technology that cannot be found elsewhere—and they can help your business—it may be to your advantage to develop some type of exclusive agreement.
- **Strategic component:** If the item or service being purchased is a strategic component to your business, you may want to ensure that you have a consistent source of supply. If there is a scarcity of supply (perhaps caused by a rapid increase in market demand, a natural disaster, or a work stoppage), it will be important that your supplier will keep providing you with these components. We experienced this very situation when the supply of both stainless steel and brass components became very limited, in part due to increased demand from China.
- **Reduced cycle or lead times:** It may be important to work strategically with suppliers where collaboration can dramatically reduce cycle times or lead to another significant advantage.

Leveraging Supplier Knowledge—International Markets

On the international front, our stainless steel supply partner provided strong support as we explored options in China. They had built a new factory in Shanghai several years earlier in anticipation of the rapid growth in the Chinese manufacturing sector. They were in a position to provide us with the same quality of stainless steel strip in China that we worked with in the United States. Unlike other Chinese steel companies, they could ensure the consistent quality that was essential in our critical application. They also shared with us their knowledge of various Chinese domestic manufacturers of stainless steel tubing. This information was invaluable as we worked to understand the threat of Chinese imports and the potential importance of the Chinese domestic market. They also highlighted some of the challenges and opportunities of operating a business in China.

Equipment Design

An important part of our success was our ability to develop and design proprietary manufacturing equipment. As our sales continued to increase, we were continually looking to expand our manufacturing capacity. Rather than just duplicate our current equipment, our engineering team was always thinking about new and better ways to produce our stainless steel gas connectors. They would look at the current equipment, material, and work flow and labor steps associated with a process. They would then begin to conceptualize how it could be done better and faster without sacrificing quality. Once they had developed a concept for a new piece of equipment, they would work to identify equipment design firms that had the capabilities to build innovative equipment. We weren't just buying off-the-shelf equipment. We wanted to enhance our competitive advantage through advanced equipment design and efficient manufacturing processes.

Once our team had identified an equipment design partner, they would kick off a Kaizen (improvement) process by creating a team that included engineers and factory employees. We felt that it was extremely important to include the people who worked in the work cell in the design process. The team would analyze all aspects of the current process and identify all potential areas where it could be improved.

The team would then go about the process of developing a new and improved design. This was often an iterative process, testing out ideas and concepts and sequentially developing the conceptual design. Once this was approved, the equipment-design partner would begin the construction process. At the same time, our engineers and factory workers would design the work cell, incorporating the 5S (a Japanese workplace organization concept) concept. Once the equipment was completed, we would send a team of engineers and factory personnel to the equipment-designer partner's facility to conduct a run-off test using real materials. We would not approve and sign off on the equipment until the team gave their approval.

Before the new equipment arrived at the factory, our plant engineers, maintenance staff, and work-cell employees would work to make sure that the new floor layout had been completed. The utilities were set in place, bins for tooling were set up, work-in-process carts were readied, and signboards for performance metrics were erected. Once the machine arrived, it was quickly set in place, and the new work cell would be up and running in a few hours. All of the collaborative effort and preparation paid off in a new, more efficient work cell that was designed and developed with the involvement of our team of employees.

The end result was that we were able to successfully design, develop, and implement many different types of automated and semi-automated equipment. Several of these efforts enabled us to achieved breakthroughs and advance our proprietary technology. We integrated factory employees, maintenance folks, and our manufacturing engineers along with our engineering design firm partners to achieve these important advancements.

Lessons Learned—Supply-Chain Management

1. **A critical first step in SCM is to understand your customer's requirements and operations.**
   Visit the customer's operations and see firsthand how they run their business. This will help to identify potential supply-chain savings opportunities. Utilize tools such as voice-of-the-customer to guide your efforts.

2. **Supply-chain alliances are a critical and essential part of business success.**
   Suppliers can be a key factor in winning new business. Early supplier involvement is a critical success factor. It is important to leverage the skills, technologies, and capabilities of your suppliers. Your goal is to become a strategic ally integral to the success of your customer.

3. **Leveraging the products and services of your suppliers can create new business opportunities.**
   They may possess new products or services that may be of interest to your business. They may have experiences in related market that apply to your business. Supplier operations in international markets may create synergy for your business. Suppliers may have technical skills and knowledge that might be of value to your product-development team.

4. **Your reputation and track record can open doors that lead to new growth.**
   Companies may call because they believe that you have the knowledge and experience to solve problems. This may also pave the way for additional new opportunities. Your success will reinforce your standing as an innovator and problem solver and will help attract other new customers.

5. **Actively manage key customer relationships to prevent potential problems.**

   With personnel changes and computer system glitches, you can add value to your larger customers by proactively managing their accounts. Your customer-service team can assist their purchasing department by analyzing orders to ensure they are not in out-of-stock situations.

6. **Intellectual property protection is an important factor in SCM.**

   Suppliers may be very guarded about protecting their technology. You can work with your IP attorneys to structure the right form of confidentiality agreement.

   The ability to patent a product may be an important step in justifying the cost of a new product. With equipment design, you ideally want to own the intellectual property. It may be so confidential that you classify it as a proprietary trade secret. You will have to take extra precautions to protect the value of your equipment.

7. **Include multiple disciplines in equipment design and factory layout.**

   Include people from the work cell in the design process. Kaizen is a great method to drive improvements in your operation. Focus on continuous improvement, working to make enhancements and upgrades with successive iterations.

Chapter 9
International Market Access

This is clearly a case of European Standards being used as a technical barrier to trade.
—Wall Street Journal, *April 9, 1996*

For many years Dormont exported quick-disconnect gas connectors throughout Europe to multinational food-service chains, including McDonald's, KFC, and Pizza Hut. In 1989, McDonald's notified us that they could no longer use Dormont gas hoses in their British restaurants. Shortly thereafter Frymaster, a large manufacturer of deep-fat fryers, said that Gaz du France inspectors had rejected our gas hoses, which were to be installed at EuroDisney. We needed to understand what was happening and why, all of the sudden, our products were not allowed to be used in Europe.

Our investigation started with the onset of the Single European Act (SEA) in 1992, the result of new legislation that was going to create a single market within the EU that would result in free trade among the EU countries. The SEA grew from the discontent among European Community members in the 1980s about the de facto lack of free trade among them. Leaders from business and politics wanted to harmonize laws among countries and resolve policy discrepancies. A core element of the SEA was to create a single market within the EU by 1992. The SEA intended to remove barriers and to increase harmonization and competitiveness among its countries.

With the opportunity (and more importantly the threat) of a single market looming on the horizon, manufacturers in European countries began to take action to protect their turf. Because there was no harmonized EU standard, each European country began to implement individual national standards for gas hose connectors that included design standards on top of the normal performance standards.

Standards

Standards agencies and regulatory bodies develop product standards as a means of protecting consumer safety. These standards are ideally written by a group of people representing many areas of interest (e.g., code officials, safety engineers, manufacturers, and technical experts) that help to create a robust standard based on the most up-to-date technical knowledge, factual data, and industry experience. As a general rule, standards are "performance based"—that is, they set out a series of rigorous tests and experiments that determine if a product is fit for its intended use. The World Trade Organization (WTO) and other international standards agencies and trade agreement encourage—even sometimes require—that standards should be based performance standards. Here is a quote from the WTO:

> Technical regulations and product standards may vary from country to country. Having many different regulations and standards makes life difficult for producers and exporters. If regulations are set arbitrarily, they could be used as an excuse for protectionism. The Agreement on Technical Barriers to Trade tries to ensure that regulations, standards, testing and certification procedures do not create unnecessary obstacles.[1]

One method that some countries (and manufacturers within those countries) used to protect their local markets is through the use of "design standards." Design standards do not address safety requirements but deal with issues such as compatibility and material composition of a product. Design standards can be created to possess very simple requirements; for example, such a requirement might be that the plastic coating on gas hoses must be colored yellow. The design requirement can also be more complex, specifying the exact method of construction. One of the significant dangers of design-restrictive standards is that they may prevent better, safer, and sometimes lower-cost products from reaching the market. This ultimately hurts consumers by preventing them from having access to superior products.

---

[1]   http://www.wto.org/english/tratop_e/tbt_e/tbt_e.htm

In the absence of a harmonized European standard, any company wanting to do business in the EU would have to alter their product to satisfy each national standard. Obtaining each national standard certification is both expensive and time consuming. At that time, this could require a manufacturer to pay for fifteen separate laboratory tests and agency approvals, which could possibly require fifteen different products for exportation.

With the SEA looming, a series of new national gas hose standards were passed in countries throughout Europe. These new gas hose standards were developed by European manufacturers to protect their local markets. These standards contained "design criteria" that effectively forced Dormont out of the European market. We made urgent inquiries to the national standards authorities, both directly and through the American National Standards Institute (ANSI), regarding these standards. We were told that foreign companies had no standing to suggest changes or to provide technical information.

Our customers asked us to get our product approved in Europe. They wanted to use Dormont gas connectors in all of their locations worldwide. We needed to develop a plan. If we wanted to continue selling in Europe, we would have to apply for certification in each country and address each individual national standard.

American National Standards Institute

One of the organizations that I contacted very early on was ANSI.[2] We had worked with ANSI for many years as a member of the Gas Appliance Connector Subcommittee. My father had been a representative for over twenty-five years and served as the chairman of the subcommittee. As this process was unfolding, I asked the president of ANSI for advice. Throughout the twenty years of the Dormont case, ANSI tried to be supportive of our efforts to gain fair market access to the EU. However, they were limited to conversations and discussions with their counterparts.

---

[2] The American National Standards Institute is a private nonprofit organization that oversees the development of voluntary consensus standards for products, services, processes, systems, and personnel in the United States. ANSI accredits standards that are developed by representatives of standards developing organizations, government agencies, consumer groups, and companies. http://en.wikipedia.org/wiki/ANSI

ANSI had no power or ability to force the EU to cooperate or to operate within international trade agreements.

Dormont had been actively involved in the standards process. We understood how important standards were in the success of certain businesses. For products that conveyed hazardous gases, it was important to have rigorous standards that helped to ensure public safety. Our experience with the American and Canadian Standards Committee had always been positive. Committee members operated in an open, collegial fashion—working to promulgate standards that were in the best interests of the public. In hindsight, I was naïve to think that the European Standards Committees operated in a similar manner.

ANSI Standards Process

ANSI oversees the development and use of standards by accrediting the procedures of standards-developing organizations. ANSI accreditation signifies that the procedures used by standards-developing organizations meet the institute's requirements for openness, balance, consensus, and due process. ANSI also designates specific standards as American National Standards when the institute determines that the standards were developed in an environment that is equitable, accessible, and responsive to the requirements of various stakeholders. Voluntary consensus standards quicken the market acceptance of products while making clear how to improve the safety of those products for the protection of consumers. The American National Standards process involves:

- Consensus by a group that is open to representatives from all interested parties
- Broad-based public review and comment on draft standards
- Consideration of and response to comments
- Availability of an appeal by any participant alleging that these principles were not respected during the standards-development process

http://en.wikipedia.org/wiki/ANSI

Getting into the Game

Our contacts at ANSI and others suggested that we could impact the standards process if we started manufacturing gas connectors in Europe. As a "local manufacturer," we would have the ability to join the standards committees and become part of the process. Based on common business practices, language, and other factors, we determined that the United Kingdom was where we would start our efforts. In 1988, Dormont purchased a UK manufacturing firm to establish a "presence" within Europe. We began to pursue a dual path: (1) Could we work with the standards committee to amend the UK standard to eliminate the design restrictions? (2) Could we get our gas connectors approved by BSI based on the performance requirements in the standards?

As the owner of a British company, we were entitled to have a representative on the GSE/1 technical committee in the BSI that developed and oversaw the gas-connector standards. GSE/1 was made up of mostly British manufacturers of gas fittings and gas connectors. We believed that we could influence the standards process from within, as a UK manufacturer of gas connectors. However, we found out the other UK manufacturers that had voting control had no interest in amending the standard to be performance-based. Maintaining the "design restrictive" standard kept the Dormont design out of the UK, thereby protecting their position. UK consumers paid higher prices and were denied access to superior designs by these non-tariff trade barriers.

BSI Certification

We also pursued a parallel path, trying to earn a product approval from the British Standards Institute (BSI). BSI is the organization that sets standards for the UK. It also provides testing and certification services. To obtain certification, gas-connector hoses had to pass the requirements of the gas hose standard (BS 669). This standard includes two parts: BS 669 Part I applied to connectors in residential settings; BS 669 Part II was relevant for commercial gas hose connectors for movable food-service (catering) appliances. Both parts of BS 669 contained safety, performance, and design requirements.

At the request of our customer that wanted to install our gas hoses at EuroDisney, we submitted our gas connectors to Gaz du France for testing based on the new French standard. They sent us a report informing us that our Dormont gas hose connectors had passed all of the safety and performance sections of the tests. However, as expected, they did not pass the design section of the test. We presented the information to BSI, and they told us that we could still sell our products in the UK without BSI certification to BS 669-Part II because it was a voluntary standard. We found out that while BSI claimed that BS 669 was supposedly a voluntary standard, it turned out to be a de facto mandatory requirement.

In theory, we could sell Dormont gas connectors since formal compliance with BS 669 was not required to enter the British market. However, only certified installers could install gas appliances. Installers were required to be members of "The Council for Registered Gas Installers" (CORGI), a mandatory registration body for gas-installing businesses in the United Kingdom. CORGI, in turn, had enforced compliance with the gas-installation code (BS 6173). This installation code required that gas connectors must comply with BS 669. CORGI-registered installers faced professional liability and revocation of their license if they used products that were not BSI certified. This meant that while we could sell Dormont gas connectors in the UK, no one would buy them without BSI certification.

We met again with BSI officials to petition for changes in the design specifications so that the standards included Dormont gas hose connectors. We argued that the revision would not compromise the current safety and performance requirements of BS 669. BSI refused to alter the design requirements of BS 669 Part I and II, under the reasoning that these standards fell under the jurisdiction of the United Kingdom. It became clear to that altering the BS 669 standard was not an option; we were at an impasse. Just as things started to look bleak, the clouds began to clear, offering us a new possible new opening for market access.

New Path—CE Mark
In response to repeated requests from our customers, we decided to find some way of acquiring approvals for our connectors in Europe. The cost of designing and certifying different connectors for each national market was prohibitive. A more rational approach appeared to be to use the harmonized EU standards. This would enable us to sell a connector that

met the performance and safety requirements commonly accepted for these types of products.

In 1992 the European Union (EU) created a number of directives that harmonized standards in different product areas. The directives provided guidelines regarding the CE mark—which was a "declaration of conformity." Through these directives, the European Union harmonized the standards of all member states. A difference in the EU standard was that only safety and performance standards, not design standards, were used when testing products. The CE mark would show that the product met all of the requirements stated under the directive and could be sold in all member states.

The CE mark provided a window of opportunity to finally get certification and regain market access. This certification would allow Dormont to sell our product to all countries in the European Union. The European Commission authorized six notifying bodies to review applications for CE approval on harmonized products. We spoke directly to members of the European Commission, who told us that we could resolve our issue by obtaining a CE mark, thereby certifying that Dormont gas hoses were in accordance with the Gas Appliance Directive (GAD). In hindsight, this was another important lesson. I trusted the directors of the European Commission, taking them at their word. In hindsight, I should have asked for their written assurances about the CE mark.

We spoke to several notified bodies regarding the CE mark certification process and ultimately selected BSI. After consultation with representatives of the European Commission, BSI decided that Dormont's products should be tested under the Gas Appliances Directive. The scope of the GAD was restricted to appliances burning gaseous fuels used for cooking, heating, hot water production, and refrigeration. The GAD covers mainly common consumer and commercial products, including fittings. BSI included a requirement that we had to have an ISO 9000 Quality System Registration in addition to our product-testing approvals.

BSI tested our commercial and residential gas connectors to the performance criteria of BS669 Parts 1 and 2. Our connectors passed all of the required safety and performance tests, and we were issued a CE mark for the commercial connectors in September 1993. The CE mark for residential connectors was not issued at that time and was subsequently withheld pending resolution of the issue. As part of the approval process, we were required to have our quality system approved to ISO 9000 by a European registrar, a requirement not part of most of the national standards. At this point we started to market our products throughout the EU, exhibited at several trade shows, and began setting up a European distribution network.

Competitors Block Our Market Entry

In late 1993, the French authorities decided that the CE mark as issued by BSI was unacceptable. Gaz du France said that they would not recognize a CE mark issued by BSI. Needless to say, we were shocked and greatly disappointed. We had worked in good faith with the European Commission and with BSI (a notified body that is partially funded by the UK government) to obtain the CE mark.

Our EU competitors began to pressure their representatives in Brussels to take action to "protect" their business. They could not challenge the testing of BSI, which validated that the Dormont gas connector exceeded all of the safety and performance tests for the application. Rather, they created an argument that would provide the market protection that the local companies were after. In addition, the other EU certification agencies were upset with BSI because their CE mark threatened the revenue stream created by national approvals.

After much discussion, the European Commission concluded that gas connectors were not covered by the scope of the Gas Appliance Directive. The EU authorities informed the British government's Department of Trade and Industry (DTI) that, in the opinion of the Commission Services Working Group /Gas Appliance Directive Advisory Committee, gas connectors "fell outside of the scope" of the Gas Appliance Directive. They stated that BSI was wrong to issue a CE mark in this case and that member states were free to impose their own design-restrictive national standards. In December 1994, DTI informed BSI that it must withdraw the CE mark from Dormont's gas hose connectors.

Once again we lost access to the European market. The result of this was the cancellation of all orders and the elimination of the need for our European distribution network. We attempted to do everything correctly, according to the rules. Our products were safe and met the performance and safety requirements, and yet we were not allowed to sell in the European market. After our hard work and significant financial investment, we were back to ground zero.

Seeking Legal Assistance

As a first step, we knew that we needed to hire legal counsel in order to understand what, if any, actions could be taken. We hired a firm in Washington, DC, to help with the US government and in one Brussels to help with the European Union. Upon advice from our counsel in Europe, we filed a complaint with DG XV. We had already received approval and were selling our gas connectors in the UK and Belgium. The complaint claimed a violation of Articles 30 and 36 of the Treaty of Rome (dealing with mutual recognition and the free flow of goods within the union) and the mutual recognition clauses as developed by the Cassis de Dijon case law. This also addressed the principle of mutual recognition. The court held that there are no valid reasons why a product that is lawfully marketed in one member state should not be introduced in another member state.

Absent from the design restrictions, the national product standard of each country was sufficiently similar to warrant mutual recognition under Article 30. Because the UK has approved our products for sale, the products should, by the provisions of these articles, enjoy the freedom of circulation within the entire European Union. As we came to expect from the EU, our complaint was dismissed. We had numerous meetings with Senior EU officials to discuss this matter. In addition, top US officials, including our EU ambassador, personally looked after our complaint. Once again, the EU competitors had the patience to wait out our representatives, knowing that these US officials would only be in Europe for a few years at most.

United Kingdom

Our European counsel believed that the UK was in violation of several of its World Trade Organization (WTO) obligations. We wanted to prove that the UK was violating the Technical Barriers to Trade (TBT) Agreement of the WTO:

Article 2.1: Members shall ensure that in respect of technical regulations, products imported from the territory of any Member shall be accorded treatment no less favorable than that afforded to like products of national origin and to like products originating in any other country.

Article 2.8: Whenever appropriate, Members shall specify technical regulations based on product requirements in terms of performance rather than design or descriptive requirements.

Upon advice from our counsel in the United States, we drafted a 301^3 petition to address the failure of the UK to address the issue of design-restrictive standards. Initially, they told US representatives in our embassy that BSI was a voluntary body and had no relationship with the UK government. We then pointed out to them that the Health and Safety Executive (HSE), under order from the Queen, provided funding to BSI. This encouraged the UK Department of Trade & Industry (DTI) to get involved. At the next meeting of the GSE1 Gas Connector Standards Committee, in attendance were representatives of the UK government and US embassy to observe the proceeding. The veil of secrecy had been lifted, and the local UK manufacturers would now have to give proper consideration to a performance-based standard. They were no longer able to use a design-restrictive barrier to protect their local market positions.

Over the next eighteen months, we attended six meetings in London. We had to present extensive technical information to amend the standard. A considerable amount of time was spent developing a performance test for the plastic coating on the gas hose. The committee members wanted to exclude the use of polyvinyl chloride (PVC) as a suitable material for the coating. This coating is used to keep grease and dirt of the metal and allow

---

3   Section 310 of the 1974 Trade Act is commonly referred to as Super 301. As enacted, Super 301 required the USTR to issue a report on its trade priorities and to identify priority foreign countries that practiced unfair trade and priority practices that had the greatest effect on restricting US exports. The USTR then would initiate a Section 301 investigation against the priority countries to obtain elimination of the practices that impeded US exports, in the expectation that doing so would substantially expand US exports. http://en.wikipedia.org/wiki/Super_301

for easy cleaning. Once again, they were focused on design restrictions rather than performance tests.

We worked with an engineering firm to develop a performance test for the coating that addressed the concerns of the committee. Finally, we were successfully in getting the UK standard for catering connectors (BS669: Part 2) changed to be a performance-based standard. Without the help and pressure from the US government, the BSI would have continued to stonewall us (just as the rest of Europe did). We submitted our products for test certification, our products were approved and we received the BSI Kitemark. We were able to affix the label on our gas connectors, and finally we were back in business in the UK. After being locked out of the UK market for ten years, Mechline reestablished Dormont's number-one position within six months.

In order to build support for our case and encourage the US government to take action, I met with a reporter from the *Wall Street Journal* in our offices in Pittsburgh. We spoke several additional times over the course of several months. On April 9, 1996, an article first appeared in the *WSJ Europe* entitled "Hitting a Wall: US Firm's Troubles in EU Trade Highlight a Lack of Integration, Hose Maker Finds Its Efforts Largely Blocked as States Set Questionable Standards, Challenging a National Cartel?"

US Government

Based on the negative impact on American jobs, I worked diligently over fifteen years to enlist the support of the government to help establish a level playing field. I contacted, corresponded with, and met with many top officials at both the US Department of Commerce and the US Trade Representative. In fact, one former official (Helen Delaney) wrote an article in the ASTM News (8/8/1996) about the debacle entitled "Stacking the Deck in Europe: One Company's Story."

We were told that the US government supported our position. The design restrictions present in the standards were a non-tariff trade barrier and represented a violation of the General Agreement on Trades and Tariffs (GATT). The US government tried to work bilaterally with the European Commission to seek commission action to require member states to change their product standards, removing the restrictive design requirements. In spite of all the efforts, the US government did not have the political will to force the rest of the EU to level the playing field in the gas-connector category. There was little that the Ambassador could do without the support and leadership of Congress and the threat of sanctions. The Europeans were masters of delay and obfuscation. They knew that US officials would lose interest or return home soon, so delay was in their best interests in order to maintain the status quo.

In order to present the Dormont case, I was invited to participate as a delegate to the Trans-Atlantic Business Dialogue (TABD) in Charlotte, NC. This was a meeting of leading CEOs and executives from major corporations through the United States and Europe. It also included many prominent government officials. I was asked to make a presentation and review the twists and turns of the Dormont case. I received many thoughtful responses from other participants that had experienced trade issues.

In a broader context, there are many other small US firms whose story is similar to Dormont's, with the same devastating results. I would encourage Congress to ensure that we have effective processes in place to address these issues. In addition, we need to put in place metrics to measure the performance of the USTR and Commerce in issue resolution. Just like a business, their performance should be measured and they should be required to justify their budgets based on achievement of predetermined goals. As a final thought, the Dormont case became widely known in the field of international standards. The Monterrey Institute of International Studies developed a business case study entitled "Designed to Regulate? A US Manufacturer Seeks Entry into the EU Market," which is being used is various business schools.

Lessons Learned—International Market Access

1. **Our US international trade policies and legislation are not aligned with economic reality. In the absence of substantive policies and programs that support USA companies, our manufacturing base will continue to decline.**

   The Dormont case was an example of how US products are denied fair access in international markets, and yet we allow those same countries to freely sell in our country. There are also numerous examples of how international governments subsidized specific industries, encouraging local employment and creating an uneven playing field.

2. **I was naïve to think that the European Standards Committees operated in the best interests of consumers.**

   I believed that the European Standards Committees would operate in an open, collegial fashion, working to promulgate standards that were in the best interests of the public. It became clear that many committee members were there to protect their own commercial/national interests.

3. **It is important to get written commitments from government officials.**

   Senior EU officials told us that we could resolve our market-access issues by obtaining a CE mark. We relied on their advice and guidance to address our EU market access hurdles. When our EU competitors fought to have our CE mark removed, these diplomats developed a case of selective amnesia. If we had their guarantees in writing, we may have been able to fight the unwarranted revocation of our CE mark.

4. **US businesses need to press Congress to ensure that there are strong safeguards and sanctions that prevent our trading partners from denying fair access to their markets.**

   This is particularly true for the European Union. It was frustrating when we would compete against the subsidiary of a European company in the American market—and at the same time they worked to deny us fair access to their local market. Our government needs to take concrete actions to prevent international companies from taking unfair advantage of the United States.

5. **The USTR and Department of Commerce need to develop performance metrics, including their performance on issue resolution.**

   The performance of government agencies should be measured, and they should justify their budgets based on achievement of predetermined goals.

Chapter 10
Selling the Business

It's the chance of a lifetime, in a lifetime of chance,
And is high time you joined in the dance.
—Dan Fogelberg

Over the course of my years at Dormont, I had heard many stories about business owners who successfully sold their businesses. I was a member of an organization—the Young Presidents Organization (YPO)—that conducted seminars on how to proceed with this process. And through our acquisitions, we had developed some experience in this arena. I knew that if we were thinking about selling Dormont, I would have to become more knowledgeable about the process and that we would need to put together a team of top-notch advisors. There were risks and pitfalls along the way, including the time that it would take away from running the day-to-day activities of the company. As much as I thought I knew before we started, I quickly realized that this was much more challenging, complex, and emotional than I had imagined.

Factors Impacting Sale Decision
There were several factors that led to the decision to investigate the possible sale of the company. These included the upward trend of activity in mergers and acquisitions, current and emerging business risks, and the desire for financial diversification for our family.

The first reason was the significant strength of the financial markets and the opportunity that it presented to a seller. The financial markets were quite strong in the early 2000s, and this was driving an increasing number of mergers and acquisitions (M&A). There were several things driving the chase for deals, including the growth of hedge funds, the desire of pension funds and mutual funds to increase returns through alternative investment strategies, the strength of the dollar, and the ongoing need of publicly traded companies to increase sales and profits. This meant that there were a lot of dollars chasing a limited number of deals, thereby driving up purchase price multiples. The race for deals was making the market more and more attractive for sellers. In addition, the strong dollar made acquisitions for international companies more attractive. I had heard of several deals for manufacturing firms where the owners had received double-digit multiples for their companies.

The second reason involved the risks and areas of concern for our business. Over time, some of these become more or less important. At that time, there were four areas of significant concern:

1. **Business Consolidation**: As a result of the strength of M&A markets, we began to see a number of companies (customers and suppliers) start to get swallowed up by larger entities. On the customer side, we saw companies like Home Depot purchasing a number of catalogs and distributors to build and expand their wholesale business. We saw Ferguson Enterprises (a large plumbing wholesaler in the Southeast USA) purchase Familian (Western USA), thereby creating a plumbing wholesale juggernaut.
    Another growing trend saw the creation of a number of "roll-ups," where a financial company would purchase several distributors around the country and roll them up into one entity. Their goal was to create a regional or national entity and reduce costs through the elimination of duplicate overhead, more efficient business processes, and greater leverage with suppliers. After a roll-up was announced, as a supplier one could expect the new entity to "demand" lower prices (to help offset their acquisition costs). One response to the growth of these larger businesses was the continued growth and development of "buying groups," which allowed a number of independent distributors (sometimes as many as fifty to one hundred) to join together to negotiate more favorable terms (i.e., lower prices) from their suppliers. This provided them with a combined purchasing power that enabled them to compete with these new, larger organizations.

Finally, we saw the large retailers, such as Lowe's and Home Depot, continuing to grow at a rapid pace. This was putting significant pressure on traditional wholesale distribution and forcing many smaller companies to close. And as you expect, the bigger the retailers became, they more they began to demand from their suppliers.

2. **Line consolidation**: A second significant trend was a concerted effort by companies to reduce their number of suppliers. This would enable them to purchase from fewer vendors, thereby reducing transaction costs. For Dormont, this put us at risk in our residential business because we had a limited line of products. Several of our competitors offered a broad range of plumbing supplies, making the gas-connector category ripe for a consolidation effort.

3. **Product-Liability Litigation**: One of the unfortunate aspects of conducting business in America has been the exponential growth in litigation. This was especially true in our line of business. While the number of incidents was extremely small and we had an impeccable record, the growth in the number of lawyers encouraged the increase in litigation. In almost every case that we dealt with, the incident was a result of human error, typically caused by the installer. In spite of detailed installation instructions and licensing requirements in certain areas, we were always amazed at what people would do. Inevitably, whenever there was an incident, a plaintiff lawyer would sue everyone possible—the installer, the appliance manufacturer, the gas utility, the homebuilder, the retailer or wholesaler, and anyone with a product that might be involved, including a gas-appliance connector. Working with our insurance carriers, we would invest a great deal of time and effort to get dismissed from suits where our products were not even involved. We worked diligently to address every single case. The risk that we saw going forward was that the number of suits and the time and cost associated with them would increase, regardless of our safety record. The plaintiff lawyers would go after deep pockets, and as a successful business, we were at risk.

4. **Offshore manufacturing**: An increasing trend in the plumbing business, among many others, was the growth of products manufactured offshore. In the plumbing world, the majority of these items were coming from China. It did not help that the

CEO of a leading retailer ordered his purchasing department to significantly increase their purchases from China, putting in place a purchasing office and distribution center in Shanghai. During my trips to China, I visited a number of companies that were making gas-connector prototypes. They were definitely targeting the US market, and this presented a significant risk to our core business. Many wholesalers and retailers were already buying pipe, valves, and fittings from China. It would have been easy for them to add gas connectors or other products to their offshore purchases.

The third reason that encouraged me to explore the possibility of a sale was the concept of financial diversification. Almost all financial planners and wealth-management advisors talk about the importance of having a diversified portfolio, using an asset-allocation model. By that, they mean that an individual, family, or other entity with a significant amount of assets can protect the value by investing in an array of financial instruments, including equities (stocks), bonds (fixed income), and possibly other types of alternative investments (real estate, investment funds, etc.). During my tenure at Dormont, I had reinvested everything I could back into the business to support its growth. Other than my residence and 401K, almost all of my financial net worth was tied up in the business. A sale would provide the liquidity to create a more balanced, diversified portfolio that would not have the high concentrated risks associated with being invested in one entity.

Goals/Objectives

As with any strategic initiative, I knew that it was important to define the goals of the sales process. What would lead me to agree to sell the business, and how would we measure success? As I began to think about the process, I put together a list of goals:

1. **Maximize the value of the company**: One important goal was to realize the highest possible value for the company. This was going to be a once-in-a-lifetime opportunity, and I knew that we had to get it right. I realized that using an investment-banking firm with specific expertise in this area would help realize this goal. However, there were other considerations that I needed to consider.

2. **Manage confidentiality**: We had always been very cautious and highly concerned about any confidential information concerning our business. I was very concerned about limiting the disclosure of confidential and/or strategic information in case the sale was not consummated in which case another competitor might use it against us. I knew that all involved parties would sign a confidentiality agreement, but that does not mean that you could prove later on that they did not use this information to compete against you. Many times companies look at other businesses without having any intention of buying them—they just want to learn as much as they can about their customers, products, manufacturing, financials, profit margins, suppliers, etc. Our manufacturing processes utilized proprietary technology that provided us with a competitive advantage in the marketplace. We had very attractive margins in certain areas of our business and did not want to disclose this information if it might be used against us in the future. So I was highly concerned that we manage and limit the disclosure of confidential information throughout the process.

3. **Create competition and a sense of urgency**: Presumably this is one of the key value-adds of the investment bank. They will access mutually agreed upon buyers and create a process that optimizes the interactions with both strategic and financial buyers. They want to be in a position to maximize negotiating leverage with the potential buyers as the field is narrowed. They also want to limit or minimize any surprises that might negatively impact the valuation by potential buyers. The investment bank works hard to build and sustain credibility, instilling in the buyers an honest and true picture of the company.

4. **Find the best fit for the company**: I wanted to ensure that we found a good partner, a buyer that would value the great company that we had built over the past sixty years. We did not want someone who would cut costs (slash and burn) and turn the business into simply a manufacturing facility. It was also important that the acquiring entity share many of our values, especially as it related to treating our employees well. We felt strongly that mutual trust and respect with our people was an important part of our success.

5. **Minimize disruption to the business**: We wanted to execute a process that would limit any negative impacts on the business. In order to accomplish this, we knew that we would have to limit the number of people involved. In addition, we would not discuss or acknowledge that we were considering a sale. It was important that we kept running our business in as normal a way as possible. In fact, we made several investments in IT systems, factory infrastructure, and equipment on schedule, even though it would have boosted the EBITDA had we delayed them.

6. **Represent the company with integrity**: We wanted to ensure that whoever represented our company had integrity and an excellent reputation. As our partners in the process, I knew that our advisors would be a reflection of our business.

Building an Advisory Team

Once I had made a decision to explore the possibility of selling the business, I knew that I needed to create a strong advisory team, learn as much as I could about the process, and select an investment bank to lead the process. I spoke with several friends and YPO members who had been through this process, and they provided many excellent suggestions. The key recommendation was to use an investment bank that focused on selling businesses only.

In terms of an advisory team, I knew that we would need an extremely strong team that would include legal, accounting, and financial expertise. I had developed a trusted relationship with Jonathan Schmerling, an estate-planning attorney with Cohen Grigsby LLC. Jon was someone I had complete trust in, and I knew that he would be honest and straightforward with me at all times. He was the first person I asked to be part of my advisory team.

The next step was to select an attorney. I wanted to hire legal counsel that was separate from the firm that we used for our corporate matters, and someone with significant M&A experience. Jon arranged for a meeting with Christopher Carson, one of their best lawyers in this area. I was impressed with his background, knowledge, and experience. I asked Chris to join the advisory team and to represent us in the transaction.

I also had to select someone with a strong tax and accounting background. I knew that it would be helpful to have someone who was familiar with both Dormont and my own personal financial situation. We had used the Alpern Rosenthal accounting firm for a number of years for both our business and personal requirements. I had developed a good relationship with two of their partners, Sean Brennan and Joel Rosenthal. Sean's specialty was in the tax area, and Joel had a broader range of experiences, including working with mid-market companies in the M&A area. We discussed the situation and decided that Joel would be the best person to join the advisory team. He would be able to consult with Sean about any tax matters related to our financial situation and could bring his extensive experiences to our team.

Selecting an Investment Bank

The next step was to select an investment bank to work with. This was a great opportunity to learn as much as I possibly could about selling a business—a veritable PhD course in mergers and acquisitions. I spoke to several people who had been involved in the M&A field, including a friend who had worked at Piper Jaffry. He strongly suggested that we work with an investment bank that worked for sellers only and one that focused on business with annual sales between $50 and $250 million. I knew that we could have confidentially approached some of the obvious buyers on a direct basis, thereby eliminating the investment-banking fees. I needed to understand where an investment bank would add value in the process in a way that would justify their significant fees.

I began to investigate the various investment banks that were recommended. This was a critical decision, and we had to get this right. We narrowed the list down to four firms: Harris Williams, Goldsmith Agio, Brown Gibbons, and ABC (fictitious name). The first three met all of the requirements. ABC was much larger, but I thought it would be valuable to understand if their approach differed in any way. I arranged for the first round of meetings with the investment banks and our advisory team. We had each firm sign in advance a detailed confidentiality and nondisclosure agreement that Chris had provided. The goals of the first round were to:

- Get to know the people and who would be on the deal team
- Understand the history and philosophy of the firm

- Assess their M&A experience with manufacturing firms
- Understand if they had any previous contacts with the logical potential buyers
- Ask them to describe how they would manage the sale process

Each group provided a strong overview of their firm and a good explanation of their process. It was at this point in the process that I brought Stacy onto the team. We had discussed the idea before but had never pursued it in any detail. I was concerned about how he would react to the thought of selling the business. Once I had a better idea about how it would work and the valuation range, I felt more comfortable about taking the next step. He agreed with the decision to explore our options and offered to help in any way possible. As always, he was a vital and critical part in the success of the business.

We decided to move forward with round two, which had slightly different goals than the first round. Given that we had signed confidentiality and nondisclosure agreements, we decided to provide each of the firms with detailed financial information, including audited financial statements of the past three years of historical data and a five-year forward projection. We asked each firm to:

- Discuss their valuation methodologies[4]
- Provide a baseline (expected value) and a high-end/low-end range estimate of an expected purchase price
- Review the process that they would use to market the company
- Identify the leader and members of the "deal team"

---

[4] **Valuation Methodologies**
  - **Comparison to Publicly Traded Companies:** Demonstrates how the public markets currently value minority positions in comparable companies. Analysis is adjusted to capture the control premium in a change of control transaction.
  - **Comparison to Mergers and Acquisitions:** Demonstrates how acquirers have valued comparable companies in recent change of control transactions.
  - **Discounted Cash Flow Analysis:** Used by corporate buyers to derive a value based on the entity's future unlevered cash flows, discounted as a risk-adjusted rate.
  - **Leveraged Buyout Analysis:** Used by financial buyers to derive a value that provides an adequate return on invested equity based on the entity's future cash flows and the current terms and availability of debt financing.

- Provide examples of offer books that they had produced for other deals
- Discuss their international network and ability to attract overseas companies into the process
- Provide a sample engagement letter and review their fee structure

After the final meeting, we all met to discuss our thoughts about which firm would be the best fit, including background, experience, and deal team members. We rated each investment bank based on a set of decision criteria, which included:

- Experience in the mid-market sell-side market
- Reputation/ references
- Chemistry/fit with firm and deal team
- Knowledge of the business—will they get it (our unique value proposition)
- Capability to reach international buyers
- Input from advisory team—legal and accounting
- Experience with closely held/family businesses
- Relationship with private equity groups
- Experience with manufacturing firms

You may be wondering why I am using a fictitious name for ABC. They exhibited some egregious behavior that shocked all of us. During the second meeting, the principal from ABC excused himself in the middle of our presentation in order to take a call. He said it was from a "real customer," which directly implies that we were not real customers. He also likened the sales of our business to selling a used car. Give that we viewed this as our once-in-a-lifetime opportunity, it was not reassuring that he viewed us leftovers. Needless to say, his actions led us to quickly exclude their firm from consideration. Later on in the process, our bankers spoke with a potential multinational buyer who already knew about the deal. The person from ABC had violated the confidentiality and nondisclosure agreement and told them about the deal. He had poisoned the waters for that potential buyer. Needless to say, I was livid but decided to focus on our deal rather than pursue legal action against their firm.

As part of the process, we had requested references from all of the firms. I called many of them to develop an understanding of the thoughts of their clients. We made calls to several other banks and investment firms to get an independent perspective. For the most part, the calls confirmed and validated those opinions that we had developed in our interviews with the investment banks.

We knew that we ultimately had to make a decision, so we evaluated the three remaining firms based on the criteria that we had developed. We decided to eliminate Brown Gibbons because they were slightly smaller, had less experience, and were not as strong internationally. So it was down to Harris Williams and Goldsmith Agio. In order to finalize our decision, Stacy and I decided to travel to the headquarters of each company in order to meet the principals and get to know them better. We wanted to make sure that the owners knew us and were 100 percent committed to getting a great result for us. They seemed surprised that we wanted to visit them, but this is what we had often done with key supplier partners. We wanted to get to know them personally and be able to pick up a phone at any time if we needed any help from the bank's top executives.

We traveled to Goldsmith Agio in Minneapolis where with met with one of the founders, the managing partners, Jack Helms, and several other senior executives. We were particularly impressed with Joseph Conte, the leader of the deal team. From a background standpoint, his experience as a lawyer and a dealmaker would be invaluable. They also had an impressive track record and a firm grasp of the importance of this deal.

We then traveled to Richmond to meet the Harris Williams cofounders, Hiter Harris and Chris Williams. Bill Roman and Phil Ivey from the Boston office joined us. They had attended the Pittsburgh meetings. We continued to be impressed by their understanding of our company, their commitment to helping us achieve a superior result, and the overall strength of their deal team. They had the strongest network of affiliated bankers in Europe and Asia, a factor that proved to be decisive.

With both firms, we discussed whether they had prior experience with any of the larger US companies that would be logical buyers. We spent a good bit of time discussing their international partners and their experiences in bringing European and Asian buyers into the deal process. From the knowledge that we had gained throughout the process, we knew that an important part of the value that the investment bank would bring to the deal was their ability to attract and bring highly interested and qualified buyers into the bidding process. Given the strength of the dollar and the relative attractiveness of US companies, we thought the participation of potential international buyers would help drive up the purchase price.

This proved to be an incredibly difficult decision. We knew that it was critically important to the success of this once-in-a-lifetime opportunity, and we desperately wanted to make the right decision. We consulted with our advisory team and evaluated the strengths and weaknesses of each firm. In the end, we knew that either firm would do a great job. We decided, based on the overall strength of the deal team and the international network, to select Harris Williams.

Fee Structure

The next step was to review and execute the engagement letter. This marked a turning point in the process. We were no longer talking about the sales in academic turns. We would start spending real money and investing a significant amount of time. We wanted to make sure that we got this agreement right, and we relied upon Chris's expertise. We had reviewed the proposed fee structure from all of the firms during our selection process and found them to be quite comparable.

The typical M&A deal sell-side fee is structured with several components:

- **Monthly retainer fee**: a fee to engage the bank—typically $10-15,000/month
- **Expenses**: travel, deal book production, etc.
- **Success Fee**: by far the largest component. The key to a successful fee package is often the negotiation of an optimal success fee that drives mutually beneficial behavior.

As is standard in most deals, there was a success fee equal to 1 percent of the value of the company for the agreed-upon expected (baseline) value of the business. This was based upon a weighted average using multiple valuation methodologies. It also represented a multiple times our most recent EBITDA. In other words, we would pay the 1 percent of the sales price for a successful deal if we sold the business at the expected (baseline) value. For example, a $100 million dollar deal would result in a success fee of $1,000,000.

Given the desire to maximize the price (among other considerations), the success fee typically includes an incentive if the investment bank is successful in delivering a higher purchase price. This incentive might be structured to provide an additional 2 percent fee for a price between 100 and 120 percent of the value, plus 3 percent up to $130 million and plus 5 percent thereafter. For example, a $120 million dollar deal would result in a success fee of $1.4 million = [($100,000,000*1 percent) + (20,000,000*2 percent)]

Purchase Price	Success Fee
$100,000,000	$1,000,000
$120,000,000	$1,400,000
$130,000,000	$1,700,000
$140,000,000	$2,100,000

In hindsight, one significant lesson learned is to have a complete understanding about the expected baseline value for the business. Is the baseline value, for determining the success fee, an absolute number—or is it a multiple of the EBITDA? One of the steps in the development of the deal book is to review your financial statements for "adjustments" that will result in a higher EBITDA. These are expenses that will not carry forward to the acquiring company and may include one-time business or personal expenses. The financial statements for the deal book are then revised to show a higher, adjusted EBITDA to prospective buyers. You want to make sure that the baseline price is determined by the adjusted EBITDA. In addition, there may be "adjustments" that occur in the time frame between the signing of the engagement letter and the completion of the deal. You want to be very clear about how these adjustments will be handled vis-à-vis the success fees. After the sale, this became a significant area of tension. I wish that we had been more specific in our engagement letter on this important topic.

After one final gut check, we finalized the engagement letter and prepared to kick off the process. Ready or not, we were about to embark on a challenging, rigorous, and emotional journey

The Sales Process

The sales process included three phases: Phase I: Preparing to Market; Phase II: Marketing the Company; and Phase III—Closing the Transaction. Harris Williams had provided timing estimates based on previous transactions, assuming all went according to plan. They estimated that the process would take six to nine months. As one might expect, it is not often that everything falls into place.

Phase I: Preparing to Market
Conduct due diligence

The first step was for the Harris Williams team to gain a comprehensive understanding of our company through on-site visits with management. This would enable them to become educated advisors and to effectively convey our company's story to the marketplace. We provided them with an extensive amount of information which they used to begin drafting the all-important confidential information memorandum (CIM).

Initially, I spent a great deal of time doing a data dump with the HW team. We reviewed in detail our information, including marketing and sales brochures; customer, supplier, and internal PowerPoint presentations; intellectual property; an overview of the manufacturing processes; customer summaries by channel, geography, and business unit; key supplier information; new growth opportunities; explanation of past performance; rationale behind future projection. I also sent samples of our products and marketing materials to their offices in Boston.

The next step was to take them through the factory so that they could see firsthand our unique and proprietary manufacturing processes. I told our folks that they were from another YPO company, friends of mine who were in town and wanted to visit our factory. I walked them through each and every step in the process, emphasizing how unique it was. I highlighted the proprietary technologies that we had developed and discussed areas where we had integrated lean manufacturing and Six Sigma techniques into our production. I wanted them to understand our unique technology, which was truly a one-of-its-kind opportunity for a prospective buyer. We also went into our supply-chain management strategies, including key suppliers and methods we employed to increase turns and limit our investment in inventory.

I reviewed with them the strength of the "Dormont brand," emphasizing how well known and established our products were in the markets that we served. For example, many multinational food-service chains had specified our products by name in all of their commercial kitchens. The quick-disconnect gas connector was known as the "Dormont" or the "Blue Hose" in the food-service industry. In addition, we had developed a number of value-added solutions for appliance manufacturers that had been integrated into their products. We discussed each of our business units, our relative competitive position, and our situation in each of our channels of distribution. We reviewed our pricing strategies, promotional programs, credit policies, participation in multiple-distributor buying groups, retail programs, and OEM (original equipment manufacturers) customers. The breadth and depth of our distribution, including a broad and diverse customer base, further added to the value of the business.

We discussed the history of the company and key milestones over the almost sixty-year history. We reviewed our organizational structure, the strengths and weaknesses of our management team, and our internal administrative processes. We delved into our quality-management systems, our ISO 9000 registration, our many product certification and approvals, and the relevant codes and standards that governed our products.

During the investment bank selection process, I had the opportunity to review the CIM by the investment-banking firms. We all agreed at the time that the Harris Williams books were a cut above the rest, so I was looking forward to seeing how they would integrate all of our information into a clean, concise, and effective CIM.

Their goal was to analyze the information received during due diligence and craft a comprehensive marketing document. The CIM needed to highlight the strengths and mitigate the weaknesses of the company. They wanted to present it in a way that buyers would read it and think that the company was so special, so unique, and so valuable that they had to own it.

We wanted them to believe that they needed to prevent their competitors from acquiring the company, including its proprietary technologies and tremendous customer goodwill.

One of the challenges that we faced with the CIM was to carefully draft it in a way that would prevent disclosure of competitively sensitive information. Throughout the entire process, we were extremely careful about what information was shared and with whom it was shared. We even developed separate letters and CIM books for certain potential buyers, always being conscious of the possibility that the information could be used against us.

Together we went through at least ten iterations of the document, continuing to refine and revise. Stacy and I did most of the work at night and on the weekends, making sure that it was completely sealed off from the business. We incorporated various pictures, charts, and diagrams that would hopefully strengthen the story. I also provided draft copies to my father and our advisory team for their comments and suggestions. We wanted to produce an attractive document that would generate a strong interest from selected potential buyers.

Select group of potential buyers
The next important step was to develop a list of prospective purchasers. At first, we developed a list of "strategic buyers"—operating companies that might have an interest in the business. This included competitors, suppliers, large customers, plumbing product or food-service equipment manufacturers, gas utilities, and companies that might be looking to establish a position in the markets that we served.

The Harris Williams team put together a detailed list of "financial buyers," including a large number of private-equity groups, hedge funds, pension and insurance funds, and other clients that they knew about or had worked with in the past. We were surprised at how many potential financial buyers existed. We hoped that it was a good sign that there would be a high level of interest in a well-managed, profitable, and successful business.

Finally, we worked with their international network of investment bankers to develop a list of potential offshore buyers, including a wide range of companies in Europe and Asia.

We discussed with the Harris Williams team the sales-process alternatives relating to the type of marketing process that they would employ. We needed to consider various factors including the "confidence in the valuation" and the "speed to close." On the one hand, a broad marketing process would result in a large and diverse universe of buyers. This would create the largest number of alternatives but would slow down the time it took to close the deal. Speed can be a critical factor in some situations, where the value of the business might be diminished if the knowledge that it is for sale becomes publicly known. This might have a negative impact on customers, suppliers, and employees. The longer the sales process the greater the probability that the information is leaked, in spite of your best efforts.

On the other hand, a targeted marketing process with a limited number of buyers will create a streamlined process. This should speed up the time to close. However, it may limit the opportunity to introduce potential buyers into the process that might drive up the sales price. It might also exclude potential buyers who might bring a creative idea that might be interesting to the seller. While this process may take longer, it might be worthwhile to explore a wide range of options, particularly if speed to close is somewhat flexible.

Ultimately, we selected a broad marketing process with several important modifications. We reviewed and approved the final list and provided thoughts on companies that were to be contacted. We also identified any competitively sensitive buyers that were on the list. We excluded companies where we felt that the competitive risk was too great. There were a few companies that we did not trust, regardless of any confidentiality agreement that they might sign. Their behavior in the marketplace and our experience with their senior management affirmed our decision. While they might be willing to make an attractive offer, we agreed that we would never want to work with or for them.

For a few other companies that were competitors or potential competitors, we revised the initial introductory letter and pulled out certain information. We were also extremely careful with any customers or suppliers. Where appropriate, I made a call in advance so that we minimized any issues, concerns, or disclosures by these companies.

Phase II: Marketing the Company
Quickly and effectively market the company

We worked with the Harris Williams team to develop an initial letter of interest, a two-page document that briefly described the company. We were now ready to go live with the process. The HW team began to contact each prospect and asked for a quick response. A CIM was sent to interested parties *only after they had signed a confidentiality and nondisclosure agreement.* There were a few companies that wanted to modify the agreement, but we accepted only a few minor changes. The HW team maintained contact with parties reviewing the CIM while keeping us informed of the status of each prospective buyer. It was exciting to see the high level of interest; each day would bring news about the list of potential buyers that we had so carefully put together. We were particularly interested in certain strategic buyers that we thought would have a high level of interest.

Evaluate preliminary indications of interest

The initial marketing period concluded with all of the interested parties submitting preliminary indications of interest in written form. This included an indication of value and how they would operate the company within their structure. At this point, there were close to fifty companies that expressed a level of interest. It was probably split two to one in terms of financial buyers to strategic buyers. However, we were quite pleased with the absolute number and strength of the companies. The Harris Williams folks knew most of the financial buyers, and they were thrilled with the response. Based on a set of decision criteria that we had developed, including the indications of value, we mutually agreed upon a group that would be invited to visit the company.

Conduct management visits

We discussed at great length the number of companies to invite for a management visit. Based on their experience, the HW team knew that for each visit it took a significant amount of time and energy to prepare and conduct the meeting. The typical number of invited companies is approximately three to five. However, there were a number of interesting potential buyers in the mix, and we wanted to know more about them. We decided to invite nine companies in for the next step in the process. Working with the HW team, we prepared a management presentation that we would present to prospective buyers.

An extremely important (and incredibly time-consuming) step is the creation of a data room. We worked very closely with Harris Williams and our legal counsel in the formation of a data room. We decided to use a virtual data room (VDR), which is an Internet site (using a secure log-on supplied by the vendor that can be disabled at any time by the vendor if a bidder withdraws) to which the bidders and their advisers are given limited and controlled access. Much of the information released was confidential, and restrictions were applied to the viewers' ability to release this to third parties by forwarding, copying, or printing. Digital rights management was applied to control information and is the highest level of technology available to do so. Detailed auditing was also provided for legal reasons so that a record was kept of who had seen which version of each document as well as when and for how long.

For our virtual data room, we had to gather up every relevant document related to the company, including contracts and agreements relating to customers, suppliers, employees, legal activities, and certain financial and tax records. Each document had to be scanned, numbered, and entered into the VDR. We had to do all of this while trying not to raise any suspicions among our employees. This proved to be one of the most challenging parts of the process.

We then scheduled nine meetings over a three-week period. It was important to keep them in close proximity and to continue to move forward with the process. We worked with the HW team to choreograph each visit and to prepare a presentation binder for each meeting. We carefully reviewed the biography and company background before each meeting. We wanted to understand their motivation behind the acquisition and if there were specific topics that we might emphasize that underscored the value for their organization.

I reserved a suite at a local hotel for a two-week period so that we could leave our materials there. We wanted to create a "stage" in the room that would incorporate a series of visual aids that would support the presentations. These included a trade show booth, several point-of-sale displays, a table of product samples, and twenty poster boards that were mounted on four different easels. We also had an array of marketing and sales materials available.

The visits were similar in terms of the time structure. After a few meetings, it began to feel like the movie *Groundhog Day*, where each day kept repeating itself. We had to make sure that we maintained a high level of energy and were fresh for each meeting. The potential buyers did not know how many meetings we were holding. They only knew that there were other suitors who were interested. The teams would fly in the night before the meeting, and we would have dinner at a private room in downtown Pittsburgh where we could conduct a confidential conversation. This was a great opportunity for us to get to know each potential buyer. We were going to be on the next day, but that night we were able to ask questions about their business and their background.

The next day we would meet early in the morning in the hotel suite. On several occasions, the folks invited additional people who represented mezzanine finance companies. We would take about four hours to diligently walk through our presentation. We would then have lunch brought in and answer additional questions. After lunch, we would all drive out to the factory. We asked everyone to dress in business casual clothes, because we did not want to alarm any of the employees. I told folks that there was a YPO meeting in Pittsburgh and that we were going to be bringing a few folks through for a factory tour. In almost every case, we limited the number to two people on a tour, which took about ninety minutes. We would then go back to my office, along with one of the HW team members, to answer any additional questions. Now that the management meetings were completed, we moved to the next step in the process.

Phase III: Closing the Transaction
Solicit and evaluate offers
The groups that had attended the management meetings were asked to submit formal proposals for the company. One extremely important step was that our legal team (led by Chris Carson) drafted a stock-purchase agreement (SPA) in advance. We asked all of the suitors to review and provide a marked-up copy with their proposal. The SPA includes many provisions that can significantly affect the value of a deal. These include factors such as the representations and warranties, a basket and cap for post-closing issues, and other matters that might jeopardize the deal. A cleaner agreement provided a greater probability that the deal would be closed in an expeditious timeframe.

It was critically important to simultaneously negotiate the SPA with the financial offer, especially when you still have leverage in the negotiations. The Harris Williams folks suggested that the companies do a "light markup," meaning that we wanted to see only a minimal number of changes to the SPA. In addition, we asked each group to explain how they would manage the company going forward and what role they saw for our management team.

Once all of the written offers had been received, we sat down with the Harris Williams team to analyze the alternatives. They also conducted due diligence on the offers—working to better understand the structure of the proposed deals, the time to close, and any other outstanding issues. They presented their summary along with recommendations regarding strategies to further enhance the chances of a desired transaction.

Negotiate and close the transaction

We were now entering a critical phase of the process. The role of the investment bank was to facilitate and lead negotiations to achieve the best result, including price, terms, and timing. We had developed the following set of decision criteria to help us differentiate among the nine offers.

1. Purchase price/structure of offer
2. Probability of closing
3. Ongoing role for company management
4. Impact on employees
5. Details in purchase agreement—reps and warranties, escrow, environmental, legal
6. Impact on business—strategic vs. financial buyer
7. Chemistry with buyer(s); how would they manage the business after the sale

We ultimately narrowed it down to three potential buyers—one was a strategic buyer (Watts Water Technologies) and two were financial (private-equity) buyers. Based on the criteria that we had developed, we all agreed that the Watts would be the best fit. After a great deal of soul searching, I called the president of Watts and told him that we had a deal. We still had to schedule several meetings to review and agree upon the final details in the stock-purchase agreement. Our legal team did a great job and helped us make it through these challenging discussions.

As part of the agreement, Dormont would operate as a separate subsidiary of Watts. Stacy and I, along with the rest of our management team, would continue to run Dormont. All of our employees were retained, and there were no changes in compensation or working conditions. They wanted us to continue to grow profitably and build Dormont. Given the potential that some companies are dismantled after an acquisition, we knew that this would be a relief to our employees and other stakeholders.

Once we had a signed agreement, one of the first steps that would take the most time was that we needed to submit the proposed deal to the Federal Trade Commission for approval. This step was a requirement for certain acquisitions under the provisions of the Hart-Scott-Rodino Act. We did not think that there would be any issues, but we needed their sign-off before we could proceed. Our lawyers worked with the Watts general counsel to prepare and submit the required paperwork and documentation. We received the approval in early December.

We worked with the Dormont and Watts management teams to develop a communications plan. We crafted a common message and then tailored it to the different target audiences—including employees, customers, suppliers, manufacturers' representatives, and trade publications. We held several meetings and made numerous phone calls throughout the month of December. We wanted to reassure folks about the value of the acquisition and the continuity of operations. The sale was finalized on December 28, 2005. As a thank you to all of our wonderful employees, we paid a special bonus to our employees based on their years of service. They had all played an important, vital, and essential role in our success—and we wanted to make sure that they knew how much we appreciated all of their hard work, dedication, and commitment.

Post-Sale Process

Stacy and I were both asked to join the Watts senior management team. We would fly to Boston once a month and became active participants in their leadership. It was interesting being back in a large corporate environment again. It also became clear that there was a significant amount of change that would be required to improve the operating performance of the company.

I was asked to lead the development of the Watts corporate strategy. Building on the work that we had done at Dormont, I took previous board presentations and began to update them and add additional structure. Our goal was to update the existing strategic plan for the upcoming board meeting, and then we would embark on a more structured planning process in the summer.

We were asked to lead the efforts to evaluate several acquisitions in the food-service area. In another interesting twist of fate, we immediately began working on a deal to purchase a company in the food-service space. We were now on the other side of the deal as the potential acquirer. Having just been through the process was incredibly helpful in understanding how it worked and what we were looking for. We met with the president of Watts and developed a list of twelve projects that would drive the synergies of the acquisition and further integrate Dormont with the various Watts companies. Each project was interesting and substantial and provided the opportunity to create additional value.

After I had been working for Watts for about six months, I began to think more and more about my family. One of my hopes was that the sale of the business would allow me to spend more time with them. However, the opposite was happening. In addition to running Dormont, I was now actively involved in developing the strategic directions of a multinational corporation. Our daughters were entering their senior year of high school, and we had begun the process of looking at colleges. I knew that in slightly more than a year they would be off to college—and our lives would never be the same. While on a family vacation I spent a great deal of time thinking back over the past twenty-five years. Tracy and the girls had always been great in allowing me to travel extensively and put in whatever time was needed to grow our business. I was now in a position where I could spend more time with them, especially over the next twelve months. After many lengthy discussions, I decided to resign from Watts. I did not know where life's journey would take me next, but I was happy and grateful to be able to be at home during our daughters' last year of high school.

Lessons Learned—Selling the Business

1. **Interview multiple firms when selecting an important product or service partner.**

   This process provides you with a great opportunity to learn more about the business sphere where they operate. You will be provided with a wealth of invaluable information that will make you a more informed consumer. You will also be able to ask more detailed questions and compare and contrast the style, content, and processes of the companies vying for your business.

2. **Working with a dedicated sell-side investment-banking firm may significantly increase the ultimate purchase price.**

   The reason to hire an investment-banking firm is for the knowledge, expertise, and ability to successfully execute the sale process. While this may be your first or second time through the process, they have completed hundreds of deals. They understand how to manage the process and will help keep your emotions in check. It will also allow you to continue to manage your own business, an extremely important factor during the sale the process.

3. **Negotiating the stock-purchase agreement with final contenders may be critically important in minimizing the risk of closure.**

   We were able to ask for minimal markups to our stock-purchase agreement while we still had negotiating leverage. Proposed changes to the SPA from potential buyers can significantly impact the value of the deal. In addition, how they handle the process may be indicative of both the final negotiations and your future relationship. This process flushed out areas of concern where buyers sought to shift risk.

4. **Legal counsel became increasingly important toward the end of the process.**

   The drafting of the stock-purchase agreement defines the detailed financial aspects of the deal, including those factors (cap and basket, reps and warranties, etc.) that can affect the ultimate purchase price. It also starts to spell out the role that you and your team may have in the future entity. Your legal team will be highly involved in reviewing and discussing every proposed change to the SPA. Once we had selected a final buyer and agreed in principal on a purchase price, the role of the investment bankers grew smaller.

5. **It is extremely important to consult and work closely with your advisory team throughout the process.**

   We kept our lawyers and accountants connected to the process at every step along the way. We had discussed in detail all of the potential tax implications of various deal structures and had run financial analyses to understand the net impact. The advice and guidance of our team of experts was a critical part of our success.

6. **The process will take more time and energy than you anticipate.**

   It will be a significant challenge for you to simultaneously manage the business and the sale process. The time required to work with your bankers, lawyers, and advisory team, getting comments and input at each step along the way, can be substantial. In addition, developing the electronic data room took much more time than I would ever have imagined. It highlighted areas where documentation was not up-to-date or sufficient. The breadth and depth of document requests, covering all agreements or contracts in every area of your business, will be significant.

7. **Maintaining confidentiality becomes increasingly difficult.**

   We worked extremely hard to keep the entire process as confidential and quiet as we possibly could. As we began to spend more and more time in meetings and we asked for documents that were needed for the data room, people began to grow suspicious. This reached its height during the management meeting phase, when we were out of the building in the morning and back in the afternoon for a series of factory tours.

8. **It is important to understand what you want in the future.**

   Private-equity firms will want you to roll your proceeds back into the business and sign a contract to realize a "second bite of the apple." You will need to be clear on what you want to do in the future and how you will feel working for another company. You are no longer in charge, which will be a huge change for you. You will also want to think through the potential impact on your employees, customers, and suppliers.

Appendix/Resources

Chapter 1: New-Product Development

- *Winning at New Products: Creating Value Through Innovation,* Robert G. Cooper, Perseus Books, USA, 2011.
- *Product Leadership: Creating and Launching Superior New Products,* Robert G. Cooper, Perseus Books, USA, 2000.
- *Lean, Rapid and Profitable New Product Development,* Robert G. Cooper, Product Development Institute, Canada, 2005.
- *Acquiring, Processing, and Deploying: Voice of the Customer,* M. Larry Shillito, CRC Press, USA, 2001.

Chapter 2: Strategic Growth

- *Improving Performance: How to Manage the White Space in the Organization Chart,* Alan P. Brache, Jossey-Bass, USA, 1995.
- *How Organizations Work: Taking a Holistic Approach to Enterprise Health,* Alan P. Brache, John Wiley & Sons, USA, 2002.
- *Implementation: How to Transform Strategic Initiatives into Blockbuster Results,* Alan P. Brache, McGraw-Hill, USA, 2006.
- *The Art and Discipline of Strategic Leadership,* Mike Freedman, McGraw-Hill, USA, 2003.

Chapter 3: People: The Foundation of a Great Organization

- *Career Architect Development Planner,* Michael M. Lombardo and Robert W. Eichinger, Lominger International, USA, 2010.
- *Lominger/Korn Ferry Leadership,* www.lominger.com (website).
- *Making Change Happen One Person at a Time: Assessing Change Capacity within Your Organization,* Charles H. Bishop PhD, AMACOM Books, USA, 2001.

- *PSP Metrics*, www.psp-hrd.com (website).

Chapter 5: International Partnerships

- *Lean Thinking: Banish Waste and Create Wealth in Your Corporation*, James P. Womack and Daniel T. Jones, Free Press, USA, 2003.
- *The Machine That Changed the World: The Story of Lean Production*, James P. Womack, Daniel T. Jones, and Daniel Roos, Free Press, USA, 2007.
- *Harvard Business Review on Doing Business in China*, Harvard Business Review Paperback Series, Harvard Business School Press, USA, 2004.

Chapter 7: Customers

- *The Power of Pricing*, Michael V. Marn, Eric V. Roegner, and Craig C. Zawada, (Article on McKinsey website: download. mckinseyquarterly.com/popr03.pdf)
- *The Price Advantage*, Walter L. Baker, Michael V. Marn, and Craig C. Zawada, Wiley Books, USA, 2010.

Chapter 8: Supply-Chain Management

- *Supply Chain Management Review*, www.scmr.com (website).
- Council of Supply Chain Management Professionals, www.cscmp. org (website).

Chapter 9: International Market Access

- *Hitting a Wall: US Firm's Trouble in EU Trade Highlight a Lack of Integration, Hose Maker Finds Its Exports Largely Blocked as States Set Questionable Standards, Wall Street Journal Europe*, Timothy Aeppel and James Pressley, April 9, 1996.
- *Designed to Regulate? A US Manufacturer Seeks Entry into the EU Market.* Center for Trade and Commercial Diplomacy, Monterey Institute of International Studies, Monterey, California, http://www.commercialdiplomacy.org/pdf/case_studies/gas_pressure_valves.pdf

- *Stacking the Deck in Europe*, Helen Delaney, ASTM News, 1995.

Chapter 10: Selling the Business

- Harris Williams: www.harriswilliams.com.
- Cohen Grigsby: www.cohenlaw.com.
- Alpern Rosenthal: www.alpern.com.

About The Author

Evan J. Segal is no stranger to success. Having driven growth in both small and large businesses, and having worked to improve management efficiency in both the public and private sectors, Mr. Segal has a unique perspective on the challenges businesses face—and on the economic and political trends that often underlie them.

A business executive with extensive management experience, an entrepreneurial aptitude, and the proven ability to compete in a global marketplace, Mr. Segal has a strong record of performance in creating jobs, introducing innovative ideas, and building successful teams. Mr. Segal's commitment to growth and ability to think creatively served him well as the President and Owner of Dormont Manufacturing Company, the inventor and leading manufacturer of flexible stainless steel gas appliance connectors. Dormont, a global manufacturing business, developed products used in multinational foodservice chains and sold in leading appliance retailers and distributors throughout the world.

In a challenging business environment, Mr. Segal led the dramatic growth of Dormont. He quickly built and managed high-performance teams, implementing a series of best practices and scalable world-class management processes. Mr. Segal was active in leading industry trade associations and has been a speaker at numerous conferences and industry events. He served on the Board of the National Association of Food Equipment Manufacturers and was a member of the Young Presidents Organization.

Mr. Segal has also worked to make government more efficient, bringing his management acumen and innovative thinking to his role as Chief Financial Officer at the United States Department of Agriculture (USDA). Nominated by President Obama and confirmed unanimously by the

United States Senate, Mr. Segal served on The White House Innovation and Information Policy Task Force and the Federal CFO Council.

Mr. Segal graduated from the CMU Tepper School of Business with a B.S. and a MBA. He later served as an Executive-In-Residence at the school, where he delivered a series of lectures to Executives and MBA students. Mr. Segal is active in the philanthropic world and has served on the board of local and national non-profit organizations. Evan and his wife Tracy are the proud parents of two wonderful daughters.

Evan currently serves as the President of Smart Management Lessons, serving as an author, public speaker, management consultant and corporate director. Please contact him directly if you would like to discuss any of these opportunities.

For more information:
Email: evanjsegal@gmail.com
Website: www.evanjsegal.com
Facebook: www.facebook.com/EvanJSegal
Twitter: @evanjsegal
LinkedIn: www.linkedin.com/in/evanjsegal